SARATCHANDRA CHATTOPADHYAY'S

# THREE CLASSICS

The New Arrangement (*Naba Bidhan*)
Pointing the Path (*Patha Nirdesh*)
and
Bindu's Son *(Bindur Chhele)*

Translated from the Bengali by
JADU SAHA

SHIPRA

ISBN: 978-81-7541-403-0

First Published in India in 2008

*Saratchandra Chattopadhyay's Three Classics*



*Published by :*
**SHIPRA PUBLICATIONS**
115-A, Vikas Marg, Shakarpur, Delhi-110092 (India)
Tel. : 91-11-65277210, 22500954, Fax : 91-11-22458662
Email : info@shiprapublications.com
www.shiprapublications.com

*Dedicated to*

*Abhijit Ghosh (New Delhi)*
*Shyamal Gan (Kolkata)*
*and*
*Sonny (Atlanta)*

## *Introduction*

### I

Saratchandra Chattopadhyay was born on September 15, 1876, in Devanandapur, a village in West Bengal. His father, Motilal Chattopadhyay, was educated but because of his bohemian nature, he could never keep a job for long. This resulted in financial difficulties for the family, which were somewhat alleviated by the patronage of Saratchandra's maternal grandfather, an affluent man living in Bhagalpur, Bihar. The shelter provided by Saratchandra's grandfather to Motilal and his family during their times of financial stress lasted only for a few years, however, as the grandfather died when Saratchandra was sixteen.

Saratchandra's basic education alternated between the school in his native village and one in Bhagalpur. He passed his Entrance exam from Bhagalpur school in 1894 but further education stopped altogether a year later when his mother died and the family fell into dire poverty. At that time Motilal was living in a suburb of Bhagalpur but away from his in-laws' home. Talking about himself later in his life Saratchandra said:

> "*My childhood and youth were passed in great poverty. I received almost no education for want of means. From my father I inherited nothing except, as I believe, his restless spirit and his keen interest in literature. The first made me a tramp and sent me out wandering the whole of India quite early, and the second made me a dreamer all my life.*"[1]

About his father's 'keen interest in literature' and its impact upon him Saratchandra said in the same quotation:

---

[1] Quoted from the Introduction to *Srikanta*, Part I by Kshitish Chandra Sen and Theodosia Thompson, Oxford University Press, London, 1922 and quoted in *Sarat Sahitya Samagra,* Ananda Publishers, Calcutta, 1993.

*"Father was a great scholar, and he had tried his hand at stories and novels, dramas and poems, in short, every branch of literature, but never could finish anything. I no longer have his work — somehow it got lost; but I remember poring over that incompleteness. Over (and over again) in my childhood, for many a night I lay awake, regretting their incompleteness, and thinking what might have been their conclusion if finished. Probably this led to my writing short stories when I was barely seventeen. But I soon gave up the habit as useless, and almost forgot, during the long years that followed, that I could even write a sentence in my boyhood."*

Like the proverb, "every cloud has a silver lining", Saratchandra's poverty in his early youth also had a bright side. While living in poverty in Khanjapur, a suburb of Bhagalpur, he came into contact with a number of people interested in literature and literary activities. Anupama (later changed her name to Nirupama) Devi, author of *Annapurnar Mandir,* and her brother, Bibhutibhusan Bhatta held regular literary get-togethers in their home, which were chaired by Saratchandra. The other members of these gatherings were Rajendranath (Raju) Majumdar, and Saratchandra's young maternal uncles, Surendranath, Girindranath and Upendranath Ganguli. Raju is said to be the dare-devil Indranath in Saratchandra's masterpiece, *Srikanta* and Upendranath would later become the editor of the Bengali magazine, *Bichitra.* These people played significant roles in launching Saratchandra's literary career.

Meanwhile, Saratchandra alternated between petty jobs and what he called *tramping* as a wandering ascetic between 1895 and 1902, and totally gave up writing stories as a *useless habit.* However, just before his departure for Rangoon, Burma, in 1903, his maternal uncle, Girindranath, convinced Saratchandra to send his story, *Mandir,* for the *Kuntaleen* literary competition. Saratchandra was not in the least interested in it but after much cajoling by this uncle and other friends he agreed to send it in the name of Surendranath Ganguli. Sri Jaladhar Sen, the veteran editor of *Basumati* magazine, judged *Mandir* as the best story of one hundred-fifty odd submissions. *Mandir,* supposedly by Surendranath, became the first story of Saratchandra published. Encouraged by his success, Saratchandra continued to write in the magazine, *Jamuna,* under three different names: his own, Anila Devi (his elder sister) and Anupama.

This magazine turned out to be the catalyst to revive Saratchandra's literary career. It propelled him into fame while he was living in Burma and he returned to live in Calcutta in 1916. In the introduction to the English translation of *Srikanta,* mentioned earlier, he said about the second and glorious phase of his career:

> *"A mere accident made me start again, after the lapse of about eighteen years. Some of my old acquaintances started a little magazine, but no one of note would condescend to contribute to it, as it was so small and insignificant. When almost hopeless, some of them remembered me, and after much persuasion they succeeded in extracting from me a promise to write for it. This was in the year 1913. I promised most unwillingly, perhaps only to put them off till I returned to Rangoon and could forget all about it. But the sheer volume and force of their letters and telegrams compelled me at last to think seriously about writing again. I sent them a story for their magazine, Jamuna. At once it became popular, and made me famous in one day. Since then I have been writing regularly. In Bengal, perhaps, I am the only fortunate writer who has not had to struggle."*

While living in Bhagalpur Saratchandra befriended Sourindra Mohan Mukherjee, who later got his novella, *Baradidi* (The Elder Sister), published in 1903 in *Bharati*, one of the most influential literary magazines of that time. It was published in three installments, while he was living in Burma. The author's name was kept secret in the first two installments to heighten suspense and readers' interest. The editor of a competing magazine was convinced that the writer was none other than Rabindranath Tagore. He showed the first installment to Rabindranath and told him of his suspicion. The poet, already established as a world-class story writer, said that he hadn't written it and added that it was the work of a *powerful writer.* The third installment revealed the name of the "powerful writer," to be Saratchandra Chattopadhyay, making him a celebrity overnight. He kept on writing and sending a steady stream of novels and novellas for magazines in Calcutta. Some of them had their origin in his Bhagalpur days but were reworked. However, the majority of the stories were new and written in Burma. The second phase of his writings from Burma (1903-16) is considered to be his spontaneous work and it is also most popular. Included in the works of this period are such masterpieces as *Baradidi, Birajbou* (Biraj, the housewife), *Sreekanta, Charitrahin* (The Immoralist), *Devdas, Parineeta* (Espoused),

*Palli Samaj* (The Rural Society), *Ramer Sumati* (Ram's Turning Around), *Bindur Chhele* (Bindu's Son), *Patha Nirdesh* (Pointing the Path), and *Niskriti* (Deliverence). These would earn him he title, "The Immortal Wordsmith."

In the third and last phase of his writings, from his return from Burma in 1916 until his death in Calcutta on 16 January, 1938, Saratchandra wrote many novels, novellas, and short stories. Notable among the novels of this period are *Svami* (The Husband), *Grihadaha* (House of Ember), *Bamuner Meye* (The Brahmin's Daughter), *Dena Paona* (Debts and Dues), *Naba Bidhan* (The New Arrangement) and *Shesh Prasna* (The Last Question).

Besides fiction, Saratchandra wrote many critical essays on social and political issues of his time and dramatized three of his novels. Notable among the essays are *Nadir Mulya* (Worth of a Woman), *Svadesh O Sahitya* (Motherland and Literature), and *Bartaman Hindu-Musalman Samasya* (The Hindu-Muslim Problem of Our Time). The last one, though not politically correct, is as relevant today as it was at that time. The views expressed by Saratchandra would be echoed decades later by the Nobel Laureate, V.S. Naipaul, in his book, *Among the Believers.*

Saratchandra actively participated in the freedom movement. He was president of the Howrah District Congress Committee and an associate of the great leader, C.R. Das. He also came in contact with Netaji Subhash Chandra Bose. In his novel, *Pather Dabi,* (Call of the Road), Saratchandra sympathetically portrayed armed struggle against the British Raj by the Bengali diaspora living in Burma. It was published in 1926 and it was soon confiscated by the British Government and banned until 1939. The idea presented in his fiction became a reality during the Second World War when Netaji Bose organized his Indian National Army after the fall of Singapore. His army marched through Burma into the North-eastern part of India, raising a tidal wave of freedom movement in India after the fall of Japan.

## II

Saratchandra spent his literary career when his contemporary, Rabindranath Tagore (1861–1941), India's Poet Laureate, was always in the limelight. The literary scholars acclaim Rabindranath as the best writer in Bengali language. But Saratchandra's glorious achievement is that he continues to be the most popular and best loved Bengali writer, outshining even Rabindranath in mass appeal. The outlooks of these two literary giants couldn't be more different in many respects. Rabindranath came from a wealthy and aristocratic background. As the poet humbly wrote:

> *"I don't find the entrance door everywhere.*
>
> *My station in life stands as the barrier.*
>
> … … … … …
>
> *In a tiny corner, ever isolated by fame*
>
> *In society's crest, seated at a narrow window I remain.*
>
> *Sometimes I have been to the courtyard of the other side*
>
> *But never had enough courage to venture inside.*"[2]

Rabindranath painted the big picture in his novels and dealt with lofty and metaphysical subject matter. Rabindranath, the father of Bengali short stories, wrote about half of his ninety-two short stories between 1891 and 1995 for the magazine, *Sadhana,* started at his initiative. Saratchandra was living in Bhagalpur during this time and he was unaware of Rabindranath's short stories.

Bankimchandra Chattopadhyay (1838-94), considered to be the father of modern Bengali prose writing, established new artistic and intellectual standard for Bengali literature. He was a master stylist and his language was powerful and compact. His genius was in writing powerful romantic novels, the storylines and characters often coming from the pages of history. Bankimchandra was not attracted to writing short stories. Saratchandra was familiar with the works of Bankimchandra and he was influenced by him. Saratchandra's language was even closer to spoken Bengali, a trend started by

---

[2] *The Flute: Selected Poems of Rabindranath Tagore*, Translated by Jadu Saha, Shipra Publications, Delhi, (2003) p. 261.

Bankimchandra. With the exception of a few short stories, Saratchandra penned mostly romantic novels and novellas, but none of the characters or stories was historical.

Saratchandra, with his lower middle class background, knew poverty firsthand. Many of his novels, novellas and short stories paint it in great detail, almost with pathological accuracy. His carefully crafted, at times frighteningly real characters and events captured the late nineteenth to early twentieth century Bengali society. These writings also plumbed the depth of Bengali middle class psyche like no other writer before or since. His encounters with life as a country youth gave him the inspiration, ingredients and storylines for his life-like characters in simple settings. The strength of his stories lies in the utter simplicity of his writing style and the control of every detail of his characters. The distinctive features and the essence of purpose he gave to the characters made them more attractive and perhaps larger than life.

The characters of his stories and novels and novellas came from his personal experience. He created them in his own inimitable style. The inspiration, ingredients and storylines for his characters in the (often) uncomplicated family settings came from his encounters with life as a country youth. His heroes act on impulse, can appear wavering, indecisive, and even petulant. Pathos in many of his stories takes the reader through an emotional roller coaster ride which is not easily forgotten. However, Saratchandra's stories usually have happy endings. In this respect they are as sweet and satisfying as fairy tales.

He gave graphic descriptions of social malaise, often giving a subtle reformist twist in depicting the social scene. But he refrained from value judgment and suggested no solutions. He felt that as a writer it was his duty to raise awareness of the issues. Remedial action was the work of social reformers.

In his acceptance speech in a meeting to celebrate his fifty-seventh birthday at the Calcutta Town Hall on 15 September, 1933, Saratchandra said the following about his inspiration:

> *'My literary debt is not limited only to my revered predecessors. I am forever indebted to the people who give this world everything they have and get nothing in return, to the weak, deprived and oppressed people whose tears nobody cares to notice, to the helpless people whose lives are filled with*

*misery and who never even have the time to think why they have nothing while there is abundance of everything around them. Their pain and suffering inspired me to speak. They made me take up their cause and plead for them. I have seen endless injustice done to these people, unfair and intolerable iniquity. That is why I primarily write about them. I know that spring come to some in this world with its beauty and bounty, with the cuckoo's song and the southern breeze laden with the perfume of myriad flowers. But they remained beyond the pale where my sight remained imprisoned forever. I never had the opportunity to come close to them This deficiency is abundantly apparent in my writings.*"[3]

Saratchandra's writings attest to the truthfulness of his above remarks. Furthermore, his sensitive and respectful portrayal of women and his romantic stories make Saratchandra a much loved writer. His women characters are either lovers or mothers and they come from all walks of life — from the well educated and sophisticated *Brahmo* diva of Calcutta, to a rustic housewife with little or no education or even a prostitute. He not only accurately depicts Bengali society as it was in those days, but also excels at presenting complex human emotions and relationships.

## III

There are a few recurring motifs in Saratchandra's writings. He, along with Rabindranath, was among the first to give women a voice in his works (Usha in *The New Arrangement* and Hemnalini in *Pointing the Path* in this book). We also find men in love suffering from lingering illnesses and their beloved women nursing them back to life (see *Pointing the Path*). Woman is cast in mother's role.

Another common theme in his stories is sacrifice, which transcends desire and acts as a redemptive force. Women most often bear the burden of this sacrifice. But Saratchandra speaks equally eloquently of the discontent of that sacrifice. This is at the root of ambivalence in his heroes. This contradictory amalgam of the conservative and the provocative is a staple in Saratchandra's fiction

---

3 Translated by the author from the speech in *Sarat Sahitya Samagra,* Vol. 2, Ananda Publishers Private Ltd., 1993, pp. 2117.

and we see its manifestation at many levels in these two works of fiction in this book.

To understand these two novellas in this book in the context of their time, a bit of social history is helpful. In Saratchandra's time, a Hindu could have more than one wife, though it was not common, except among the *Kuleen* Brahmins (highest of the high caste) in Bengal. There was no social or scriptural taboo against polygamy until it was prohibited by the Hindu Marriage Act in 1955. Child (arranged) marriage was also a common practice at that time as was the practice of dowry. Though it has been banned by law, giving dowries continues unabated in many parts of India to this day.

So it is not surprising to see Shaileshwar, the hero of *The New Arrangement,* marry a child bride, Usha, before his departure for England for higher studies and then his father sending Usha back to her parents' home over some squabble about dowry. Shaileshwar returns home, becoming Anglicized in his way of living, abandoning his first wife and marrying another woman of similar background as his. Divorcing the first wife was not necessary according to the Hindu practice of the time. When the second wife died and Shaileshwar wanted to marry for the third time, it didn't even occur to him that his first wife was alive, until one of his friends pointed it out to him. By bringing her back into Shaileshwar's household, Saratchandra creates the ambivalent amalgam in the plot, which is the staple of many of his stories.

One more aspect of social history of the time is worth mentioning. Shaileshwar's and his brother-in-law, Kshetramohan's way of living and their world-view depicts a section of Calcutta society that made T.B. Macaulay's dream come true when he advocated making English as the medium of post-secondary education in India.

> "*We must at present do our best to form a class of persons, Indian in blood and colour, but English in taste, in opinions, in morals, and in intellect.*"[4]

---

[4] From Thomas Babington Macaulay, "Minutes of 2 February 1835 on Indian Education," *Macaulay, Prose and Poetry,* selected by G.M. Young (Cambridge MA: Harvard University Press, 1057), pp. 729.

This is how some repatriated Indians, were in the late nineteenth century and early twentieth centuries only to be swept away in the tidal wave of patriotism in the 1920s and 1930s. As mentioned before, Shaileshwar is also one of those heroes who acts on impulse, appear wavering, indecisive, and even petulant. His first wife, Usha, in contrast is just the opposite. But she bears the burden of sacrifice when abandoned by her husband and when she comes back in the end and makes the 'new arrangement' by keeping a Muslim butler. She does it because of another recurring motif in Saratchandra's stories. Woman's love and in many Saratchandra's stories flows in a tangent: the love of an aunt or a stepmother is depicted as stronger than that between the birthmother and her child. Usha is depicted as loving her stepson more than his birthmother did when she was alive. Usha makes the sacrifice for the love of her stepson and not for the love of her husband.

There is a classic rich boy – poor girl plotline in *Pointing the Path.* Both Guni and Hem fall in love soon after they meet but marriage between them is out of the question. Her mother, Sulochana, is firmly against it because Hem is a Hindu and Guni is a *Brahmo,* the Hindu reform sect which believes in one God, condones remarriage of widows and is opposed to idol worship, the Hindu caste system, and child marriage. Hem is given in marriage but becomes a widow within a year. Sulochana is remorseful to see that she has ruined the life of her daughter, who could have everything but has nothing! The ambivalence in the characters of both Guni and Hem stands in the way. Hem is tradition-bound but paradoxically empowered by a slowly but surely modernizing society. Guni loves Hem dearly but in the end he can't cross the invisible barrier of the widowhood of a Hindu woman. The realist in Saratchandra firmly maintains the balance between romance and tradition till the end and, unlike most of his other stories he does not allow romance to win over obstacles in this one. Consequently, the story has no fairy tale ending.

As mentioned before *Bindur Chhele* (Bindu's Son) was published in *Jamuna* in 1913, it was one the many stories Saratchandra wrote while he was in Burma. To understand this story in the context of its time another bit of social history is helpful: joint family was normal in Saratchandra's lifetime. All the brothers and unmarried sisters lived with one or both living parents as one family. Widowed aunts (father's sisters) and sometimes cousins too lived in the same joint family. The eldest son became the 'head of the family' after the father's death. It was his responsibility and duty to make sacrifices and look after everyone in the family.

The motif of sacrifice in Saratchandra's stories reaches almost martyrdom in *Bindu's Son.* Though women generally bear the burden of this sacrifice in other stories this burden falls primarily on Jadab, the patriarch in this story. His devoted wife, Annapurna, does her part with loving care as the mistress of the household. Considering the time and traditions of Hindu society her conduct is exemplary but not extraordinary.

Once again we see woman's love flowing easily but not naturally. It flows in a tangent: the maternal love in Bindu, the aunt, is depicted stronger than that between the birthmother, Annapurna, and her child, Amulya. The aunt is portrayed as the *real mother* and the birthmother becomes sort of a stepmother. The conflict and tension in the plot is anchored to Bindu's love and affection for *her* son and her extreme concern for his welfare. Bindu can not tolerate even a slight delay in feeding milk to her son, nor can she send him out of her sight to a primary school away from her home. While Annapurna could acquiesce to Nareen's bad influence on Amulya for the sake of keeping good relations with relatives, the mother in Bindu was outraged and crossed the limit. She directly insulted Annapurna whom she loved and respected as an elder sister and, indirectly, Jadab who was a loving father to her. Another recurring theme in Saratchandra's stories is that there is a mother in every woman. This aspect in Bindu's character is portrayed in the story so skillfully.

Saratchandra gives a graphic description of Jadab's sacrifice in educating Madhab from the latter's own lips. Saratchandra speaks equally eloquently of the discontent of that sacrifice when Annapurna lashes out at Bindu after she insults her and Jadab in a fit of anger. Though Bindu realizes that she has offended Annapurna grievously she refuses to apologize after repeated entreaties by her husband. Instead, she tries to commit suicide by starving to death. Her heart cries out for her son, Amulya, her *didi*, Annapurna and the hardship she has inflicted on her beloved, *batthakur*, Jadab. She would break but she would not bend. This appears to be nothing less than stubbornness and pride. But there is a word in Bengali language for it.

It is *abhiman* and it has no one-word equivalent in English. It means an amalgam of sadness, shame, and anger. Annapurna also has the same *abhiman* in her heart about Bindu. To give a happy ending to the impasse of two sisters-in-law, Saratchandra gets Jadab to intervene. He is the head of the family and none can disregard him in a joint family.

In the *Times Literary Supplement* of July 11, 1918 the following comments were made about Saratchandra's Bindu's Son:

> "*Our ignorance about India is limitless. Recently a European, using Jeris as his penname has written in Blackwoods Magazine — Some people say that Rabindranath is Maupassant's equal in writing short stories. Yet there are others who think of him as better. Recently a new genius has appeared in the field of Bengali literature. Only he can be compared to Maupassant. Fortunately Mr. Chattopadhyay's stories are not burdened with the dirty sexuality of the French writer. The extraordinary craftsmanship he has displayed in depicting woman's character and a child's mind is rare not only in Bengali but also in world literature. It is pleasurable to hear the simple but sweet words from the lips of women in the joint family setting in India, Bengal in particular. No other Indian writer has been so successful in painting such a real picture. No fault can be found in the conversation of his characters. They all come out life-like.*"[5]

The above comments are not far off the mark even today.

As long as people will love "love stories", Saratchandra's works will not lose their appeal or become outdated in context. That is why Saratchandra's stories continue to have such pan-India appeal to this day and have been translated into all the major Indian languages. His works were a rich repertoire of themes and emotions to stir liberal hopes and fears in the conservative people of India. Even before Saratchandra's works were translated into other languages they became a goldmine for directors from the tinsel towns and continue to be made in to new versions. Though the recent versions of *Devdas* and *Parineeta* have very little in common with the original Bengali stories, the name of Saratchandra has proved good enough for box office success.

Ottawa, Canada **Jadu Saha**

---

[5] Quoted by Sukumar Sen in Bengali in the Introduction of *Sarat Sahitya Samagra, Part I*, Ananda Publishers, Calcutta, 1993. [Translation by the author].

# The New Arrangement

*(Naba Bidhan)*

*The New Arrangement* (Naba bidhan) is not only a masterful tapestry of Anglicized Bengali society of the early twentieth century Kolkata but it also depicts a rainbow of complex human emotions and the triumph of love suffused with pain and suffering. As long as people will love "love stories" *The New Arrangement* will not lose its appeal or become outdated in context.

## *One*

Sri Shaileshwar Ghosal, the hero of this story, was a widower. He had just set in motion the idea of marrying again when he landed into an embarrassing predicament in his circle of friends. Had it not been so, it would be difficult, even to guess how this short story would have changed its course and color and where it would have ended. So it is necessary to narrate the background in the introduction.

Shaileshwar was a professor of philosophy in a prestigious College in Kolkata. He had a foreign degree and his salary was eight hundred rupees a month. He was thirty-two years old. His wife had passed away about five months earlier, leaving behind a son, who was about nine-year-old. He lived in his home in Pataldanga where his forefathers had lived for successive generations. In his household he had, apart from his son, about seven or eight servants including an orderly, a Muslim cook, a groom, and a coachman. One might say that these servants were his family.

To begin with, he didn't want to marry at all. It was natural. Now he has the desire. There is nothing new about it either. Recently, it became known that the second daughter of Bhupen Barujje of Bhwanipur had passed her Matriculation exam and that she had a beautiful face. Such interest is without any novelty at all. Yet, on that day, the topic came up for discussion during the evening tea-session in Shaileshwar's own drawing room. There was one modestly paid schoolteacher of the Sanskrit language among his friends, though not in the inner circle. His thirst for tea extract was no less than that of any high-salaried professor. The professors called him *Diggaj*, (vastly learned or sarcastically speaking, a portentous idiot) for his eccentric nature. He never gave much thought to what he said nor did he accept any responsibility for it. *Diggaj* himself didn't know any English. His whole being would be aflame with anger to hear of any woman appearing for any exam. When the topic of Bhupen Babu's daughter came up he blurted out, "You banished one wife, swallowed another and now you are talking about marriage once more! If you have to have a family again then, may I know, what is wrong with the daughter of Umesh Bhatchajji? If you want to start all over again do it with her."

The assembled gentlemen were astounded, for they had no clue to what was being said. "Since God's grace has fallen on the poor soul why don't you bring her home? But don't get into another marriage," said *Diggaj*, "Passed her Matriculation! That squares it all!" His eyes were bloodshot in anger. Shaileshwar, himself, controlling his outrage with difficulty, said. "She is insane! Don't you know it, *Diggaj*?"

*Diggaj* normally would be beside himself if someone called another person insane or lunatic. He flew off the handle in rage. "Is everybody insane?" he thundered, "People call me insane too. Does that make me insane?"

Everyone burst into laughter. But that did not sweep the matter under the carpet. When the laughing stopped, Shailesh, looking embarrassed, said by way of an explanation, "The situation with Umesh Bhatchajji's daughter was an unfortunate matter in my life. I was married before my departure for England. But there was a very serious dispute about something between my father and my father-in-law. Besides, my father could not keep her in the house because of her eccentric nature. I didn't see her after my return from England." So saying, Shailesh, with a forced smile on his face, said, "Oh *Diggaj*, the genius! If it were not so, wouldn't they have tried to send her here, even once? I have never seen you miss even one of our tea sessions. Should she come here indeed don't you ever expect any tea. Along with holy water from the Ganges and sprinkling of a mixture of cow-dung and water she would clean you all out from this place. I can assure you of that in advance."

"No, Never!" *Diggaj* said emphatically.

But no one else joined in this discussion. After a few inconsequential exchanges they all left, claiming that it was getting late in the evening. The evening sessions usually ended at about this time and that is what happened on this occasion too. But there was a pale shadow of gloom on every face, which refused to go away.

## *Two*

Shailesh understood it clearly that his friends did not approve of his marrying for the third time. Instead they had censured him with their silence. On the one hand, there was no end to his annoyance. On the other hand, his feeling of shame was also boundless. It seemed difficult for him to show his face in public. When Shailesh was married for the first time at the age of eighteen his wife, Usha, was then only eleven years old. Since the girl was very good looking Kalipada Babu[1] agreed to sell his son in the matrimonial market at a low price. Yet after Shailesh had left for England the in-laws had a feud over the debts and dues of dowry. The father-in-law had sent his daughter-in-law to her parents' home by force, so to speak. So when his son returned home he could not, on his own accord, bring the daughter-in-law back. Also, he did not have any desire to do so. On the other side Umesh Tarkalankar was also the type of a man who felt hurt, ashamed and embarrassed by it all. The proud Brahmin could not swallow his pride and that of his daughter and agree to send her, uninvited, to her father-in-law's home. Shailesh had heard something like it while he was abroad and thought that everything would fall in place after his return home. But by the time he returned home after four years, his nature and his way of life had both changed. So when the opportunity came to get married to another repatriate daughter from England, who was well-educated and well-versed in western way of life, Shailesh gave his consent in silence.

---

[1] A term of respect attached to a name, like Master or Mr. Instead of addressing a Bengali gentleman as Mr. X (the surname) it is a common practice to address as X-babu (where x is the first name). In the days of the East India Company the clerks in offices were called Babu by the British and even today a supervisory clerk is called Baro-babu. Baro meaning the big(boss).

A long time had elapsed since then. Kalipada Babu, the father of Shailesh, had passed away and the old Tarkalankar also had gone to the abode of the Manes. It was not true that no news about Usha had reached Shailesh's ears. He heard that she was living with her brothers' family, spending her time in silent prayers, worship rituals, religious austerities and with purifying agents like the Ganges water and cow dung. Even her brothers were getting fed up with her phobia of remaining pure and pollution free. None of this had pleased his hearing. But he had one consolation, that people rarely slandered the characters of such ladies. It is difficult to say how much Shailesh would have been hurt if it were so. But he had never had to hear even a whisper of any such slander.

Shailesh began to mull over the matter. For the time being he had to give up any hope for the educated daughter of Bhupen Babu. If he should bring an ill-bred, superstitious woman like Usha who was by now old, twenty-five or twenty-six, and make her the mistress of the household she would create utter chaos in everything. He had not a shred of doubt about it. He was particularly concerned about Somen. Remembering that his mother was the root cause of his misfortune, Shailesh became greatly frightened about the prospect of this woman bearing extreme malice towards his only son.

His sister lived in Shyambazar. Bibha was married to a barrister. Though his son would be well looked after there, it could not be a life long arrangement. He felt like slapping *Diggaj* across his face. He had entertained this fellow with tea and biscuits for a long time. And this was the way he returned the favor.

In reality Shailesh was not bad but he was a timid person. The embarrassment of openly doing some unseemly thing was stronger in him than doing something really shameful. Along with his pride in his higher education he had another greater source of vanity. It was his belief that knowingly he never could do the slightest wrong or injustice to anyone. He knew well that his friends might never openly say anything but in their hearts they would judge him guilty in this matter. It was impossible for him to bear such calumny.

After pondering over it all night long, suddenly a simple solution came to his mind at dawn. The whole problem would be solved if he were to send for Usha. Firstly, she would not come.

Even if she came she would flee in a few days from a *Mlechchha*[1] household with non-Hindu way of living. Then no one could blame him. He could send Somen to live with his *pishi*[2] for a few days and he himself could hide somewhere else. He was surprised why such a simple solution did not come to him much earlier. This was the right thing to do!

He took seven days' leave of absence from his college. He sent a telegram to a childhood friend in Allahabad informing him that he was coming to visit. He also wrote his sister, Bibha, a letter stating that he was sending someone to bring Usha from Nandipur. Should she come, Bibha must bring Somen to Shyambazar and that he would be back from Allahabad after about seven days.

Shailesh had a dependable cousin from his mother's side, who lived in a rooming house and was employed in a merchant's office. Calling him to his presence he said, "Bhuto, you will have to go to Nandipur tomorrow to bring your *boudi*[3] here."

Puzzled, Bhutnath asked, "Who is this *boudi*?"

"Don't you remember that you were in the groom's party? It was Umesh Bhatchajji's house!"

"I remember that very well. But we don't know one another. Will she come with me?"

"If she doesn't come, she won't," said Shailesh, "What does it matter to you? The orderly and a maid will go with you. The moment she expresses her unwillingness to come you return at once."

Amazed, Bhuto remained silent for a moment or two and then he said, "Very well, I'll go. But I hope they don't abuse me physically."

Shailesh gave him the money for his expenses and a key. "I am going to Allahabad by tonight's train. Should she come, show her the locked cupboard drawers over there. The money for household expenses is in there. It must last for one whole month!"

---

[1] A derogatory word for a non-Hindu, similar to infidel used by the Muslims about the Hindus.

[2] A sister or a cousin sister of one's father, an aunt.

[3] Elder brother's wife.

Agreeing to do that Bhutnath asked, "Very well! Why, all of a sudden, is this whim of yours, *Mejda*? Are you sure that you are not digging your own grave?"

Shailesh silently pondered for a while and said with a sigh, "I am certain she will not come. But I have to do something demanded by societal norm and acceptable as right conduct. Send a message to Shyambazar. See to it that they take Somen."

That night Shaileshwar left for Allahabad by the Punjab Mail.

## *Three*

A few days later, on one afternoon, a motorcar stopped in front of the house and after a couple minutes, a twenty-two or twenty-three-year-old lady appeared in the drawing room of the house. Sitting on the carpet, Somendra was showing pictures from a large album to his (new) *nutan* Ma. He, himself, while giving the introduction with great delight said, "Ma, *pishima*[1]."

Usha stood up. She was draped in an ordinary sari with a red border and had one or two ornaments on her arm and neck. But Bibha was astounded with her beauty.

Usha was the first one to talk. With a smile on her lips she said to her son, "You did not do *pranam*[2] to your *pishima*, my darling!"

Somen perhaps learnt to do it very recently. Quickly bending his head he finished the act of veneration by touching the shoes on his *pishima's* feet. Usha said, "Why are you still standing, *thakurjhi*[3], please be seated."

Bibha asked, "When did you come?"

"I came on Monday and today it is Wednesday — that would make three days," responded Usha, "But remaining standing won't do, dear. Please sit down!"

But Bibha did not come to become close. She had filled her heart with bitterness when she left her home. "I have no time to sit. I have lots to do," she said, "I have come to take Somen with me."

But Usha responded to this rudeness with a smile when she responded, "Then how can I stay here all alone, dear? Over there I

---

[1] A sister or a cousin sister of one's father, an aunt.

[2] An act of veneration (by a Hindu) in which a younger person touches the feet of an elder in order to be blessed by the propitious dust. Also, sometimes the simple act of folding one's palms before another person or a deity.

[3] A sister of one's husband, a sister-in-law.

raised all of my sisters-in-law's children. How can I live, *thakurjhi*, without someone by my side?" Saying which she smiled again.

Bibha responded to this smile with a tone steeped with rudeness. She called the boy close to her and said, "Your father told you to stay with me. I don't have any time to waste, go and change your clothes in a hurry. I'll have to go the New Market on our way."

Being caught between the two, the boy turned pale and with trepidation pleaded, "But Ma doesn't want me to go, *pishima*." Seeing that the boy was in a tight corner Usha quickly explained, "It is not that I don't want you to go. I meant that if you went I would be very sad if I had to live alone in this house."

The boy did not say anything in response. Coming very close to his stepmother he stood there hanging on to the edge of her sari. While playing her fingers through his hair Usha added with a smile, "I can see that he does not want to go *thakurjhi*."

Feeling insulted Bibha's face became ashen in anger and she failed to control herself in spite of her upbringing in a highly cultured society with thousands of lessons in high level etiquette, and suchlike. She said, "But the right thing for him to do is to go. And it is my belief that had you not indulged him improperly he would have obeyed his father's order."

The two ends of Usha's lips stiffened a bit, otherwise no change in her facial expression was noticeable. She said, "Even we adults can not always figure out what is the right conduct for us, dear, and Somen is only a child! And how much does he understand. Since you raised the question of improper indulgence *thakurjhi* I have raised quite a few children and I know how to handle them. You have no reason to have any anxiety on that score."

Bibha warned in a stern voice, "Then I will write to *dada*[1]."

Usha said, "Please do. Also add that I attach more weight to my order from Kolkata than his order from Allahabad. But think of it dear Bibha I am senior to you in age and in relationship as well. You can not have shame, anger or hurt feeling in this matter." So

---

1 Elder brother or cousin. It is extended to other elder men out of affection or courtesy. It is also an affectionate term for addressing grandfather or a grandfather-like figure.

saying she again smiled a little and added, "Today you were so angry that you wouldn't even sit, but I am telling you now that a day will come when you, on your own accord, will come and sit by your *boudi.*"

Bibha did not give any reply to this. She only said, "I have no time today, good bye." Saying which, she went out in a hurry. Sitting in the car and looking up she could see that Usha, with Somen, was standing still like a statue and looking at her.

## *Four*

He had only seven days leave of absence but after spending two weeks in Allahabad, Shaileshwar arrived home around noon hours on one day. In the front verandah on the ground floor Somen was very busy with sticks, papers of various colors, strings and glue. At first the arrival of his father escaped his notice. But as soon as he noticed he greeted him and with a little abashment he bent his head and sort of dived near his father's feet to do *pranam.* It was apparent from his facial expression that he had not yet become an adept in doing *pranams* to elders. Though it did not feel that bad but Shailesh was surprised. But as soon as he noticed the sticks, papers, glue and the other stuffs he asked, "Somen, what are you doing with those?"

Somen, without divulging the secret at once, asked, "*Baba*[1], why don't you say what are these for?"

His father answered, "How should I know?"

Clapping his hands, his son gleefully said, "A lamp in the sky!"

"Lamp in the sky! What is the use of a lamp in the sky?"

Somen had learnt the strange legend that very morning. He explained, "Today is the *sankranti*[2], tomorrow evening we have tie it to a long bamboo pole and raise it high, *baba.* Mother said that we have to show light to my grandfathers who are in heaven now. They will bless us."

As it was Shailesh was hot under the collar. He scattered everything around, kicking them with his feet. Rebuking Somen and mimicking him, he said, "They will bless us! All superstitions! Go and mind your studies."

Seeing his lamp in the sky, which was so dear to his heart, lying scattered all over the ground Somen was about to cry. Just at that

---

[1] Another word for father like papa, daddy for English speaking people.

[2] The last day of a Bengali month.

moment a very sweet voice from above called out to him, "*Baba* Somen! Tomorrow I'll get you a much better lamp in the sky from the market. You come to me now."

While wiping tears from his eyes Somen went upstairs. Shailesh, without even glancing in any direction, entered his study with a grim face that had annoyance etched all over it. Momentarily he rang the small bell — *toon, toon, toon,* ... But no one answered.

"Abdul!"

Abdul didn't come.

"Giridhari! Giridhari!"

Instead of Giridhari the Bengali servant, Gokul, pushed his head through the parting of the curtain and said. "Sir —"

Shailesh, in a very intimidating tone shouted, "Sir —? Have all of you died?"

Gokul said, "No Sir."

"No Sir! Where is Abdul?"

Gokul said, "Ma has given him leave of absence and he has gone home."

"Given leave of absence! Gone home! Where has Giridhari gone?"

Gokul informed him that he has also gone home after getting leave of absence.

Shailesh was dumbfounded. He asked, "Isn't there any one else in the house?"

Gokul, nodding his head, said, "Sir, all others are here."

"What for are they here? Now go away from my sight—"

At once Shaileshwar took off his shoes and taking off his coat he piled it up on the table. He picked a *dhoti*[1] from the clothes' stand, took off his trousers, and threw them, aiming at a chair, far away. But they missed their mark and landed on the floor. He threw his necktie,

---

[1] The loin-cloth worn by all respectable Hindus of North-India. It is rapped round the body, waist down, the end being then passed between the legs and tucked in at the waist, so that a festoon of calico hangs down to either knees.

collar and other stuff helter-skelter and as he was sitting on his cot a small notebook lying on the table in front of him caught his eyes — "Account of household expenses" was written on its cover. Opening it he found the perfectly good handwriting from a woman's hand — account of daily expenses: Fish so much, vegetables that much, rice and pulses so much. All of a sudden the parting of the curtain in the doorway startled him. Looking up he saw a woman was entering the room. Realizing that whoever she might be she was not any maidservant Shailesh buried his face in the account book. The lady who came in addressed him in the familiar "you" and said, "Are you going to take tea so late in the day? Then you will lose your appetite for your meal."

"I am not going to take any meal!"

"It may be so. But freshen up and come upstairs. It wouldn't be right to take bath at this improper time. But I have made some snacks and asked Kumoda to make some *sarbat*[1]. Please come."

"Let it go for now."

"I am Usha, my dear, and no tigress or a bear. And no one is going to shame you for looking at me."

"Did I say that you are a tigress or a bear?" said Shailesh.

"Then why are you staying away from me?"

"I had some work to do. Why did you quarrel with Bibha?"

"You are making it up," answered Usha, "She can never write to you that I quarreled with her."

Shailesh asked, "Why did you dismiss Abdul?"

"Who told you that I dismissed him? He hadn't been paid for a year and he was restless for going home. I paid his salary in full and sent him away on leave."

Amazed, Shailesh asked, "You have paid him in full? Then he is not coming back. Why did Giridhari go?"

Usha responded, "This is very unjust on your part. Holding them captive by not paying their salary! Don't they have their families? I have paid his salary and let him go."

---

[1] A home made popular drink made by blending yogurt and fruits like mango or another fruit or flavour.

Shailesh said, "Well done indeed! Now you can make this place the hermitage of sage Vashishtha!" He was saying this with his eyes glued to the pages in the account book. Suddenly he was startled by the entry of a large sum of money and he asked, "What is this for? Rupees 406 —"

"I have paid it to the grocer's shop," responded Usha. "Still about two hundred are owed to them. I have told them that I would pay it off next month."

Shailesh was awe struck. "I owed them six hundred?"

Usha smilingly said, "Why not? You never cleared their debt, never wanted to check the account either — so you accumulated that amount over two years."

After so long Shailesh raised his head up and looked at her. "Did you go through two years' accounts?" he asked.

Nodding her head Usha replied, "What option did I have?"

Shailesh was sitting in silence. Though she had been acquainted with him for only five minutes the pale shadow of abashment on his face didn't escape her notice. "Tell me, what are you thinking about?"

Forcing a smile Shailesh said, "I am thinking that you have already spent all the money I had. But there are fifteen or sixteen days left until the payday."

Shaking her head Usha said, "Am I a child that I didn't think of that? I won't ask you for money before another month, let alone fifteen days. But do you know what a mess you have made? The milkman was saying that you owe him about one hundred and fifty, the laundry man is owed about fifty, and only they know how much you owe to the tailors' shop. I've asked them to send the detailed account."

Shailesh was frightened. He said, "What have you done? They'll probably say one thousand is owed to them. But how are you going to pay?"

Usha, without a shadow of worry on her face said, "I didn't tell them that I would pay the entire amount in one installment. I'll pay them off in three or four months. You haven't any more debt to any one else I hope? Don't hide from me, please."

Gazing at her face steadily, he said slowly, "At the time of going to Simla for last year's summer vacation I borrowed two thousand rupees from a person against a promissory note. I haven't been able to pay even one rupee towards the interest."

Usha was dumbfounded. "It is amazing," she said, "I don't think that you will let me be free of debt in less than a year. Are there any more?

Shailesh answered, "Perhaps not. It is possible that there is a small debt somewhere. But I thought I would never be able to pay off my debts in this life."

"Do you really ever think?" Usha asked.

"Don't I think?" Shailesh retorted. "How many times have I wakened in the middle of the night with the feeling of choked breath! I can't make both ends meet with my salary. Every month it is a struggle. But don't you bewitch me! Do you really hope to repay all debts?"

All of a sudden Usha's eyes became wet. It would not be an exaggeration to say that Usha felt real pain in her heart for a husband who was almost unknown to her about half an hour back. But she laughed and said, "A fine specimen of a man you are! You got into some debt for running a household. Don't you have to pay your bills? It won't take me long to pay off this paltry sum."

"Everybody will have to go through hardship —"

Usha emphatically stated, "Not a single soul! You will probably never notice that there have been some changes somewhere."

Shailesh silently sat there motionless. He felt in his heart that a ray of sunshine was falling on him from a corner of the sky, which ha been overcast with dark clouds for a long time.

## *Five*

Many letters, in postcards and envelopes were piled up. It was well after evening when Shailesh completed reading the letters and answering them, gave cursory reading, one by one, to the periodicals and a few other little things. Looking through the parting of the curtain at the demeanor of this dutiful man, busily doing his work with undivided attention would surely evoke deep respect in the mind of any unsuspecting person.

This story does not mean to show disrespect to professors. It will suffice to mention that it would be futile to hope that just because someone is a professor, all of a sudden, another person would outshine him in deception in worldly matters. After finishing the work at hand Shaileshwar himself switched on the light, picked a heavy book on philosophy and began to read it. He behaved as if he didn't have a moment to waste. However, no one had ever before seen him doing such an inappropriate act in the evening.

Just when he was immersed in reading Kumoda, addressing him from behind the curtain, said, "Babu, Ma asked me to tell you that your dinner is served; please come."

Shailesh, looking at his watch, said, "This isn't the time for my dinner! There are still about fifty minutes left until then."

Kumoda asked, "Shall I ask her to take away the food?"

Shailesh replied, "That's the right thing to do. This confusion has happened because Abdul isn't here."

The maid went away without asking any further question. Shailesh, calling after her said, "It would be another hassle to take the food away for a while. Very well then, you can tell that I am coming."

It was not the usual dining room with table and chairs. Coming upstairs Shailesh found that the sitting arrangement was done on the floor and the food was served in the traditional national style in the enclosed verandah facing his bedroom. The ancient brass platters, large and small, bowls and glasses were scrubbed clean and given a bright shine. On three sides of a large platter different items were neatly arranged. Usha was sitting on the floor, not far away, and Somen was seated clinging to her.

Shailesh sat down on the seat on the floor and commented, "I know that you are not going to eat with me but what about Somen?"

The response came from his son, "Baba, I eat with Ma everyday."

Looking at the abundance of items Shailesh asked, "Who cooked so many items? Is it you?"

Usha replied, "Yes."

Shailesh commented, "I suppose that the Brahmin cook is no longer here. As far as I can remember I didn't leave his salary unpaid. Did you dismiss him after giving him one year's salary in advance?"

Holding back her laughter Usha said, "Sometimes servants' salaries have to be paid in advance, if needed. Only keeping it overdue is inappropriate. But the cook is here. Shall I send for him?"

Shailesh, shaking his head vigorously said, "There is no need for it. I was not pining to see him. You should allow him to cook occasionally. Otherwise it might harm him should he forget whatever he has learnt."

Only Shailesh knew how much delighted he was in sitting down to eat. Suddenly he remembered the time when his mother was alive. Drawing one of the bowls near him he exclaimed, "Fantastic aroma is coming out! *Gossains*[1] don't eat meat! They cook green jackfruit with the spices used for cooking meat and think that they are eating meat curry and euphemistically calling it *gaach-paanthaa.* My taste is not of that high class. I can tolerate ripe jackfruit but *gaach-paanthaa*[2] as a substitute for goat meat is not my cup of tea."

Usha burst into laughter. Somen didn't get the reason for her laughing. But reclining on his mother's lap, looking at her face, he asked, "Ma, what is *gaach-paanthaa*?"

---

1 A Vaishnava guru.

2 A green jack fruit.

In response Usha pulled her son closer to her bosom and told her husband, "Why don't you taste it first?"

Shailesh, taking a piece of meat in his mouth said, "No, it is the four legged *paanthaa* (goat) alright. It is delicious, but how did you learn to cook like this?"

Usha's face lighted up. "Do you think that only your Abdul knows cooking?" she quipped. My father was a worshiper of *Siddheswari*. Do you think that I am coming from a *Gossain* family?"

Shailesh said, "After eating a bowl full of this who has got the guts to say so! But I have no *Siddheswari* here. But would I be lucky enough to have it everyday."

Usha said, "Pray tell, what shortage is going to stop it?"

Shailesh said, "I can forget the grief of losing Abdul from today. But my debts —"

Usha was annoyed. "Did I tell you that I was going to pay off the debts starving my husband and son? Don't you ever utter the word *debt* again!"

"You don't have to warn me about it," said Shailesh. It is not in my nature to use the word *debt*. But —"

Usha retorted, "There is no but about it. The debt was not incurred for your eating."

"I have no clue about how it happened, Usha—"

Usha's response was, "You won't need to know it ever. For mercy's sake don't banish me again as an insane one."

With his head bent down Shailesh continued to eat in silence. Somen said, "Let us go to eat, Ma. Today you will have to finish the yesterday's tale about the *Jatai* bird. Then what did *Jatai's* son do, Ma?"

Lifting his head Shailesh said, "Whatever *Jatai's* son might have done but this son has become glued to you, I see."

Patting her son's head Usha became silent.

Shailesh said, "Do you know the reason for it?"

Usha answered, "Without his mother the child felt alone in the house. What else could be the reason?"

"It may be so. But he never got so much love and affection even when his mother was alive."

Usha's face turned red in abashment. "That is your word," she said, "Shall I get you some more meat? Well you don't have to eat more meat. But, for the love of me, you can't get up without eating these two sweets. This is your only meal in the whole day. I beseech you."

Shailesh kept on gazing at Usha's face in awe. So much loving cajoling, sincere entreaty, beseeching for eating — all these sounded to his ears like the last refrain of a song, heard long after his childhood. He himself was the only son of his mother. That very thought raised a flutter in his heart. He didn't have the strength to get up without eating the sweets. Taking a slice into his mouth he slowly said, "I don't want to do the accounting, debts and dues or debits and credits of anything or any type. I want to hand them over to you, Usha, and become free of all worries." So saying he got up from his seat.

## *Six*

Shailesh did not know how one week slipped by and another Sunday arrived. As soon as she got up from bed in the morning Usha said, "Everyday I have been telling you to visit *thakurjhi.* But you are not at all listening to me! Today you must go to *thakurjhi.* Can you imagine what she might be thinking? It seems you are really going to make it look like a feud between her and me.

Shailesh feeling ashamed in his heart, said, "The pressure of work in the college—"

Usha asserted, "I know about it. That is why you couldn't make it to her place just once on your way back from college!"

"But you don't know how tired I feel on my way home. You don't have to teach students!"

Usha laughed. "I beseech you to go today for once. If you give the excuse of teaching students even on a Sunday I am sure that Bibha will not see your face for the rest of her life. So saying she called the groom before her and ordered him to prepare the carriage. "Take the Babu to Shyambazar and return immediately after leaving him there. I have need for the carriage."

At the time of leaving Shailesh suggested taking Somen with him. With a very sour face he at once stood, leaning against his stepmother. He never showed any enthusiasm to visit his *pishima.* Remembering the last encounter, in particular, his fear knew no bounds. Usha pulling him closer to her lap said with a smile, "Let Somen stay here. He will go some other time."

Shailesh affirmed, "I see that you too have perceived his reluctance to go to Bibha."

"I guessed a little from your inclination." Suggesting this, smilingly she went upstairs with her son.

It was about two-thirty in the afternoon when Shailesh returned from Shyambazar, after taking a bath and his meal there.

His brother-in-law, Kshetramohan, with his seventeen-eighteen-years-old unmarried sister and Bibha also came along. Shailesh did not want Bibha to come along. She came of her own will. She had many gripes against Usha. She was not at all contented with merely deriding Usha to her elder brother. Her motive was to engage her ill-educated and rustic sister-in-law into a polemical wrangle and utterly humiliate her before so many people. Since she met her brother today Bibha repeatedly made many unpleasant and serious allegations to prove that by inviting this woman into the house after so many years was not only a fatal mistake but also showed deep disrespect to the memory of their departed fatber in heaven. What was the need for re-accepting the one whom their father had been forced to disown? How could she maintain her dignity when the woman could not be introduced as a relation to friends and the society at large or could not be taken to any social gathering and when she was even ashamed to address her as the wife of her elder brother?

When Kshetramohan tried to make a point or two in defense of Usha, a stranger to him, he was rebuked so harshly by his wife that he had to remain silent. Bibha had angrily told, "*Dada* thinks that I know nothing. But I keep all the information. Abdul, a long-term employee, was dismissed because he was a Muslim. Giridhari was dismissed because he was from a lower caste. It is not possible for us to keep any relationship with those who are so prejudiced about caste. No matter who becomes upset with me and how much fuss they make I'll not recognize such a person as a *bou*[1] even for a day."

Every one understood who the target of this innuendo was. Shailesh slowly began to speak: "That was not the reason. They (servants) themselves were very much anxious to go home." Bibha at once interjected to say that during the lifetime of her *boudidi* they never pined to go home. But as soon as she stepped into the house they got a fresh lease on life by fleeing.

How could one respond to such sarcasm? Shailesh maintained silence.

Bibha continued, "You may know but we can't even imagine how the housekeeping work is going on." So saying she was proceeding to go upstairs to change her clothes when she added, "I

---

[1] A married woman.

can't afford not to go to my parent's home but I don't think that we will get even a cup of tea there."

Kshetramohan had maintained his silence up to this point. He did not want to butt in an argument between a sister and her brother. Unable to maintain his silence any longer he told, "First you go there and see for yourself. If you don't get tea then you can say so."

Bibha responded, "I have seen it all. On my first visit I have understood everything from her demeanor." Having said this she left. Neither of the two men knew that there was no truth to her allegation for she neither had the time or the inclination to see anything. Kshetramohan asked, "Really Shailesh, what is the matter with you? After dismissing all the servants do you want to live like a Vaishnava mendicant couple? What are you eating these days?"

Shailesh replied, "*Dal*, rice, *luchis*,[1] vegetable curry, —"

"Can you swallow that stuff?"

"At least I am not choking on them and that is the truth."

Laughing, Kshetramohan said, "I also know that it is true. It is also true that I won't choke on them either. But the amazing thing is that we can't even admit to ourselves this truth. Have you decided to live like this forever?"

Shailesh was silent for a moment and then replied, "To tell you the truth I haven't decided anything, nor she has given me that responsibility. I have decided only this much that without her consent I am not going to intervene in her way of running the household."

Keeping watchful eye on the door Kshetramohan whispered, "Hush! I can assure you if your sister hears about it there will be hell to pay!"

Shailesh added, "Even if I have no peace on this side I have peace on the other side. I don't have to worry any more about my expenses exceeding my income. Anxiety about money all day and night, after the first fifteen days of the month worries about the next fifteen days — no more of that for me. I have been saved, my

---

[1] Round flat bread made from bleached wheat flour and deep fried.

brother, I won't have to borrow money any more. She has given me the good news that whatever I earn is enough for me."

Kshetramohan said, "Can this be true! Do you think that only you have worries about money? You are not even aware that I am up to my ears in debt?"

Shailesh continued, "I left one month's salary in the cupboard drawers when I fled to Allahabad. I told her that the money was for one month's household expenses. Never before was it enough, not even when Somen's mother was alive nor after her death when I was responsible. I thought it would be enough if she could be made to stretch it to a month out of fear. I don't know whether the servants for whom Bibha was so upset were really dismissed for being Muslim or for belonging to low caste but it is most likely that they went home gladly when they were paid one years' overdue salary. Four hundred rupees have been paid to the grocer's shop, a few ancient debts have been retired and all expenses have been recorded to the penny in a small account book. I was frightened when I asked, 'What have you done, Usha? Half of the month still lies ahead and how are we going to meet the expenses?' She replied, 'I am not a child, I've got that sense.' Kshetra, I haven't felt the slightest depravation of food under her care. Traditional rice and *dal* tastes heavenly to me. I'll breathe in contentment when my tailor's debt and the debt of the promissory note will be paid up."

Kshetramohan was about to say something but seeing his wife entering the room he stopped.

The three of them then got into the car. Kshetramohan remained absent minded all along. Perhaps not even one word of what others were saying registered in his ears.

## *Seven*

In a little while the car stopped in front of Shaileshwar's gate. Entering the house the first one they met was Somen. Sitting on the threshold he was repairing a wheel of his train compartment with the hammer used for breaking lumps of coal. Looking at his appearance not one word came out of any one of them. His forehead, cheeks, arms, chest — that is most of the upper half of his body was painted in many colors. The *Panda*[1] from Orissa at the *ghat*[2] of the Ganges has tattooed in white, yellow, and red colors the names numerous gods and goddesses including the names of Jagannath from his native land and Ram-Sita from the west.

Only Bibha commented with a smirk on her face, "You're looking splendid. May you live long, my darling!"

Shailesh felt greatly ashamed before the other two. Generally he is a man of gentle temperament. Whatever may be the circumstance he is not prone to make any ruckus. But his sister's extreme sarcasm became too much for him to bear. Giving a noisy slap on his son's cheek he thundered, "Good for nothing, rascal you! From where did you get all this? Where did you go?"

Between sobs, the only thing they could understand from Somen that had a bath in the Ganges. Shailesh, shoving him hard on his neck ordered, "Go right away and wash with soap and water. Go right now!"

The three of them entered his study. The visages of both the brother and sister were extremely grave. No one said a word for a minute or so. From Shailesh's gloomy and shameful sour face it was apparent that he never expected things to go this far. But the silent

---

[1] A Brahmin priest acting as a guide to pilgrims at holy places.

[2] A landing place, a path of descent to a river or a pond, the place of a ferry and also a quay.

solemn visage of Bibha declared the she knew it all along that this was bound to happen.

Kshetramohan spoke out. All of a sudden he said with a laugh, "Shailesh, you have raised a tempest in a teapot! How could you hit the boy! It is becoming embarrassing to be with you people!"

Bibha was dumbfounded to hear her husband speak. Giving a stern look at her husband she said, "How could it be a tempest in a tea pot? Did you take it as a child's play?"

Kshetramohan replied, "I can't deny that in my opinion it is not something extremely serious."

"Meaning what?"

"The meaning is very simple. Certainly today must be an auspicious occasion for bathing in the Ganges. Somen went along and had a bath there. I can't take it as a great sin if someone, once in a blue moon, takes a dip in the Ganges instead of a shower in the tap water."

Getting angry with her husband she asked, "And then?"

Kshetramohan answered, "What happened next was also quite natural. There are many *Pandas* in the *ghat.* One of them must have tattooed the little boy with sandalwood paste with the expectation of getting a penny or two. It is not something that calls for harsh punishment."

With the same angry tone Bibha added, "Have you thought of its consequence?"

Kshetramohan said, "It gets washed out at the time of freshening up in the evening — that is the consequence."

Bibha said, "Oh! That's all! If you had your own children would you have allowed them to do it?"

Kshetramohan replied, "It is futile to argue when I don't have any children."

Bibha, feeling hurt in her heart, responded, "Argument may be futile, I too know that sandalwood paste washes away with water but its imprint may not be erased so easily. Action must be taken thinking of children's future. Today's act was very wrong. I'll say that not once but hundred times — whatever you two may say."

Kshetramohan asserted, "Not two but I alone. Shailesh has atoned for the committed sin by slapping and shoving his son. But I did not expect that a daughter, with the lineage of the teaching profession would become a *memshahib*[1] in a day. Whatever it may be, the two of you, brother and sister, can continue with dissecting the consequences but I am off."

Shailesh was silent all this time. But looking at his face he asked, "You are off to where?"

Kshetramohan replied, "Upstairs. Let me introduce myself to *thakrun*[2]. Let me try pleading with the mistress of the house and see if she will talk to me." So saying he left without any further exchange of words.

Coming upstairs to the bedroom door he said, "*Bouthakrun*[3], *Namaskar!*"

Turning her face, Usha, seeing him pulled the edge of her sari over her head and at once stood up.

Somen, sitting near his mother, was probably increasing her workload. He said, "*Pishemashai*[4]."

Usha, pointing to a low stool nearby, said in a gentle voice, "Please sit down." Two of the drawers of the chest were wide open. There was a big pile of many kinds of clothing items on the floor, including *dhoti,* shirt, sari, trouser, jacket, tie, collar, and socks. Kshetramohan, taking his seat, asked, "What are you doing?"

Somen, pulling out a pair of socks from the pile declared, "I found another pair. Look Ma, there is only one little hole here!"

Usha, taking it from her son's hand carefully kept it aside. Looking at her way of neatly arranging different items Kshetramohan was a little puzzled. He asked, "Are you making a list of donation to an orphanage or trying to clean up a mess? Please tell me what is it that you are doing?" He came with the expectation that a new housewife with a rustic background would be overwhelmed in abashment. There was no hint of that in the way Usha was carrying

---

[1] An epithet used for a westernized woman.

[2] One way of addressing a sister-in-law.

[3] A sister-in-law.

[4] The husband of the sister of one's father.

herself. Though she did not make eye contact but she answered in a relaxed manner, "I am thinking of sending these for mending. There are so many pairs of socks I don't think that there will be any need to buy any more in another ten years."

Kshetramohan, remaining calm for a moment, said, "*Bouthakrun,* there is no one here now, so let me tell you something. After seeing your sister-in-law don't form any opinion in your mind about her husband. Looking at my appearance and outward conduct don't take me for a *Firingi.* In reality I am a Bengali. I can tell you that I don't feel like hitting anyone for taking a bath in the Ganges.

Usha remained silent. Kshetramohan added, "Let me tell you something else when no one is around. You will be doing an injustice to Shailesh if you take Somen's punishment as if he was punishing you. He is not really that worthless."

Usha didn't respond to it either. She remained standing in silence. Kshetramohan said, "Please sit down now. Don't waste your time on my account." After a moment's silence he continued, "Let me learn a little housework watching how your gracious hands work."

Usha sitting down on the floor said with a smile, "This is women's work. What benefit will there be in your learning it?"

Kshetramohan responded, "I'll answer your question some other day but not today."

Usha continued to work in silence. But momentarily she added, "This work is for the poor and the unfortunate. You will never have any need for learning it."

Kshetramohan said with a sigh, "*Bouthakrun*, Even if you make this mistake from outward sparkle of our appearance then there will be no one left in this world to understand the heartache of the likes of us, unfortunates. I wish I could keep my younger sister with you for a few days! She might be able to take some of your goodness to her husband's home."

Usha remained silent. Kshetramohan was about to say something else when the sound of many pairs of shoes were heard from the bottom of the stairs. He said, "Looks like they are all coming upstairs." From the similarity of the outward apparel of

Shailesh's sister and mine please don't think that they are cut from the same cloth."

Usha, shrugging her shoulder a little' said with a smile, "Most likely I would be able to recognize that."

Kshetramohan said, "Not likely! But certainly, I am sure of it."

## *Eight*

The footsteps that were heard at the bottom of stairs were from the shoes of Shailesh, Bibha, and Bibha's young sister-in-law, Uma. Shailesh and Bibha entered the room. Uma was behind the others. As she stepped on the threshold of the door her elder brother signaling at her with his eyes said, "Uma, leave your shoes outside."

Bibha, turning back in amazement asked, "What for? Pray tell."

Kshetramohan answered, "There is no harm in it. No thorn will prick her feet not will she stumble."

Bibha replied, "I know that. I just want to know what the need for it is all of a sudden."

"Kshetramohan explained, "Bouthakrun is a Hindu lady, Besides, It is perhaps better not to enter a respected elder's room wearing shoes."

Bibha looked at her husband's feet and found that he not only advised his sister but also he himself had done it earlier. She was aflame in anger and said, "Your respect for the elders is commendable but its excess is not healthy. If, instead of being the bedroom of an elder, it were a worship room I suppose you would have taken some cow dung to purify yourself before entering."

Seeing his wife's anger Kshetra began to laugh and then said, "I have no liking for cow dung and I wouldn't have taken it even for bouthakrun's sake but since I haven't kept up good relations with the deities I wouldn't have entered their room to disturb their peace. Well, bouthakrun, I have been in this room many times before. I seem to remember that there was a good carpet on the floor. Why did you remove it?"

Usha replied, "It can't be washed and it becomes very dirty. Besides the bedroom —"

Bibha retorted in a sarcastic tone, "Does carpet make a room dirty?"

Looking at her face Usha slowly said, "It does, dear, You may not see it but plenty of dust and grime remain hidden underneath."

Perhaps Bibha was going to protest but her husband's loud voice, all of a sudden, drowned it. He began to say enthusiastically, "Well, well, bouthakrun, it serves our purpose if we can keep the dirt under cover — we want nothing more. We are happy as long as that thing remains hidden from our sight. What do you say, Shailesh? Am I right?"

Shailesh said nothing. Bibha's outrage knew no bounds. But controlling her anger she remained silent without any argument. Perhaps there was no lack of love and affection between the husband and wife but during everyday interaction, often conflicts came to the surface. Bibha could never accept defeat in the presence of other people. It was her nature. It was for this reason that Kshetramohan would frequently admit defeat and leave in the middle of an argument to avoid escalation into a full-scale warfare. But he was not in that mood today. Understanding that in a moment Bibha controlled herself.

Kshetramohan didn't have the slightest inclination to indulge Bibha. It had become almost second nature to Bibha to find fault in others and verbally abuse them. In most cases it was no more than indecent behavior on her part. But from day one she was doggedly against this blameless wife, who for no fault of her own, having gone through untold misery, had now, by chance, found shelter in a corner of her husband's house. The evil design to drive her away from that little space was filling the heart of another husband with irritation and sadness. When he had realized in a moment that one was beyond the pale of the other in all respects there was no room for forgiveness for Bibha in Kshetramohan's bitter and aggrieved heart. It was equally difficult to disclose this feeling in their highly educated society. On the contrary, it had to be kept hidden, at all cost, under the cloak of civility.

Addressing his sister, Uma, Kshetramohan advised, "If you could spend every afternoon with this boudi of yours from a rustic background you will suffer no pain in whichever family you get married in to. This much I can assure you."

Uma, with a smile on her face, remained silent. Without raising her head Usha said, "That will be the end of her! Your society will make her a pariah!"

Kshetramohan added, "That may be so, bouthakrun. But I can bet she and her husband will live in bliss."

Shailesh, giving a side-glance to Bibha said in a mocking tone, "You don't have to bet, my friend. Your words will suffice."

In response Kshetramohan said, "In any case, she can even remember today's task, her poor husband will, at least be relieved of unnecessarily buying a new pair of socks everyday."

Bibha had been silent for some time, but she could not continue any longer. Hiding her deep seated anger she said with a forced smile, "There may not be any need to mend socks in her future household and her husband may not even want to wear repaired socks. You can't predict anything."

Kshetramohan asserted, "Of course you can. You can predict if you keep your eyes and ears wide open. An experienced captain of a ship knows the depth of the water from its appearance. As soon as bouthakrun stepped in this boat she knew that with a little carelessness the mud at the bottom would come to the surface. For this reason alone, I give you a thousand thanks. And for Shailesh even a million thanks would not be enough."

Feeling very much abashed, Usha humbly said, "Kshetramohan Babu, I don't see anything deserving thanks when I have only tried to understand my husband's situation in my own household."

The response came from Bibha. "At least it satisfies one's wish to insult his wife. Besides, the person's respect and devotion come out as a flood to see another person struggling to make both ends meet."

Usha, raising her head up, asked, "Thakurjhi, do you call it a struggle to make both ends meet if one takes action demanded by her husband's situation?"

Kshetramohan at once spoke out, "No! Not at all! No civilized person in this world can even think that. But you would better ask your thakurjhi what impulse in one's heart provokes one to prove to a husband, at all times, that his wife is worthless."

Not a word came from Bibha for a while. Like an awe struck person she looked at her husband and then at Shailesh but could not say anything. At first she could not even believe that her husband was capable of hurting her in the presence of so many people. Then gazing at Shailesh, all of a sudden, bursting into tears she said, "Dada, after this I can not come to your house any more. I am bidding you farewell forever."

Shailesh became extremely concerned. Usha, leaving her work, quickly stood up and clasping Bibha's hands pleaded, "But we haven't said anything to you!"

During this thing happening Kshetramohan left the room in silence.

Bibha freed her hand and, while wiping her tears, she said, "Since I am always bearing enmity towards you it is improper for me enter this house for any reason whatsoever."

Usha consoled her, "But such a thing has never ever come to my mind, thakurjhi."

Bibha did not pay any heed to it. In a sobbing voice she continued, "Today my husband told me clearly right to my face. Perhaps dada will say the same tomorrow. It is only courting insult to poke my nose in his new household affairs. Uma, come along if you want to go home." So saying she was on her way to downstairs when she said, "It was a great blunder to step into this house when boudidi is no longer alive." Then she went downstairs. Shailesh came down in great embarrassment. He urged her, "Bibha, why don't you sit in my library room for a while?"

Bibha, nodding her head responded, "No! But dada, please do not ever forget my boudidi. She had high hopes that Somen would go to England for higher studies and become somebody. I beseech you don't let him be spoiled. If in future he gets the type of education that I saw happening to him today, we will become social outcasts."

Being overwhelmed by her tearful sobbing Shailesh entreated her, "My darling sister, then come and sit in my exterior room. I'll be extremely hurt if you leave now in such a manner."

Tears rolled from Bibha's eyes again, perhaps at the thought of Somen's future, She wiped her tears with her sari's edge and said, "Dada, I don't want to sit anywhere. Somen is the only descendant from our father's side. Please keep sharp watch on him, dada, and don't lose yourself." Saying which, she came straight to the car and sat inside. Uma was silent all the while; even now, without saying a word, she took her seat in the car beside Bibha.

Shailesh came along at once and all of a sudden he blurted, "Bibha, it is better that you take Somen. You don't have a child of your own. You raise him the way you like."

Bibha and Uma gazed at Shailesh's face in utter amazement. Bibha said, "Dada, why are you making this meaningless proposal. You won't be able to do it and I won't allow it either."

In an uncontrollable urge Shailesh asserted, "Certainly I would be able to do it. I am giving you my word, Bibha."

With doubt in her mind Bibha said, shaking her head, "It will be good if you can do it. Then send him to me. If you don't have the means to give him higher education I am promising you, dada, that I am accepting that responsibility from today." So saying she followed Uma's eyes and found that Usha, standing silently in the upstairs verandah, was watching them. When the car left in a moment Shailesh went inside and slumped in his study. He had not the intention or the courage to go upstairs. It was no secret to him that Usha had heard every word.

## *Nine*

After setting the place for the dinner at night and sending some one to call her husband, Usha, like any other day, was sitting nor far away. Only Somen was not near her. Perhaps he had fallen asleep. Shailesh came with a very gloomy face. It was expected. It was not in Usha's nature to ask futile question. She didn't ask any question about today's incident and she was not curious to know what she didn't know. Shailesh knew this characteristic of his wife from the past few days with her. Sitting down for his meal he was incensed but not surprised. With many a side-glances he tried to see his wife's face but he was certain that Usha was deliberately not facing the light. He could not eat as much as the other days. The reason for his loss of appetite lay somewhere else. Though unasked, he offered the reason on his own accord. "One can eat unaccustomed food for a few days. Should it become a daily fare then distaste turns into torture," he affirmed.

The statement might have some polemical value but knowing that it was not true in this case, Usha remained silent. She never liked to prove with arguments that untruth was really so. But to turn a cold shoulder in silence fuels the fire of anger of the other party. So when Shailesh came to bed, unprovoked he said, "I agree that at one time I did a grave injustice to you. That is no reason to assert that now only your way is right and no one else's can work. It is nothing but coercion!"

Shailesh never used such harsh words even on the first day. Perhaps Usha was shocked in her heart but did not express it. Instead she said, "I didn't understand it."

But anger increases even more when one admits to fault so humbly.

Shailesh continued, "You should have understood it. If you want to turn our upbringing, our way of life, our beliefs and societal norm upside down and make them something like those in your parent's home it becomes very difficult for the likes of us to live. Probably I'll have to send Somen to his *pishi's* home tomorrow. What do you say?"

Usha answered, "If it is necessary for his welfare, of course, he should go."

Failing to detect any acrimony or sarcasm in her voice Shailesh was in a quandary. He was neither very clear nor firm in his conviction as to why he was doing this. But the nature of this type of weak person is that he can very quickly slide very low through the door of imaginary heartache, shame and embarrassment. After a moment's silence he said, "Yes, everybody believes that there is a need for it. I don't like discord between a brother and a sister or we become an object of ridicule in our society, for the customs, practices and superstitions we do not and can not accept."

Usha did not protest or even try to explain her side. But all of a sudden she sighed. Shailesh heard it in the silence of the room. Usha, herself, did not have any altercation; she uttered not even one word about the things that were said on her behalf. It was so true that it could neither be hinted nor could be forgotten. To prove that he was not loading the punishment for Kshetramohan's misdeeds, nor was he taking revenge, he continued, "It is necessary for the person, who has to be educated in England and live in that milieu to grow up in a similar environment. It would be wrong and injustice to the boy if he were to spend his childhood in an unnatural environment." After waiting for a few moments for a response he said, "It is a different matter if you don't have anything to say about it. Otherwise letting out a deep sigh is not an appropriate response. We have come to this decision after careful deliberation about Somen's future."

Somen was sleeping nearby. Since there was no other woman in the family, he had slept with Usha from the day she came into the house. Placing her left hand lightly and lovingly on his forehead she said softly, "Whatever decision has to be taken for your son's welfare only you will do it. Can anyone think otherwise! Very well, you do that."

The electric lights were switched off. Only an oil lamp was dimly burning in a corner. Shailesh sat up in his bed and trying to see in that faint light Usha's face on the nearby bed he continued, "Besides, she will pay all expenses for Somen's education. That is no trivial matter!"

Usha could never speak in an excited voice. Speaking calmly was natural to her. She said, "No, that can not be. I can not allow her to pay for my son's education."

Shailesh said, "That requires lots of money."

Usha replied in the same calm manner, "We will have to pay, if needed. But you shouldn't stay awake. You should sleep now."

The next afternoon, after returning from his college and club, Shailesh inhaled the aroma of cooking of some very familiar and favorite food. Being surprised he went to his study with a thrilled heart. Lifting his head Shailesh found that the person who presently brought his tea and snacks was a Muslim butler.

For dinner at night the lights were switched on in the dining room, and, looking at the neatly arranged food on the table, he had to secretly admit to himself that he was pining for this food.

He had barely finished one or two items from his dinner when Usha came and sat on a stool at a little distance.

Shailesh was in good humor. Jokingly he said, "Won't you be an outcast for entering this room? Your scriptures say the even smelling is half-way to eating."

Usha replied with a little laughter, "It is unbecoming of you. You should not be citing the scriptures that you neither follow nor recognize."

Shailesh also laughed. He said, "Well I accept defeat. I'll no more cite scripture and you too can't flee this place. However, it is certain that since I teased you yesterday I have the good fortune of tasting such delicious food today! Isn't that right, Usha? But will it cost you too much?"

Shaking her head she said, "No! Unless it is wasted no food costs much. I thought of introducing these things starting the next month. But remember only one thing — don't waste anything. The way I have budgeted in my account book please follow that. Will you do that?"

Being surprised Shailesh asked, "Why not, may I know?"

Usha could not respond at once. For a moment she fixed her gaze at the floor and then all of a sudden she looked up and locked her eyes with those of her husband and said, "This is my only request to you — please do not ask me to reverse the decision I have taken after thinking all through last night."

With tenderness in his heart Shailesh said, "I have never tried to do that, Usha. I know that your decision is worthy of you. You never waver and you should not. I am weak and you are strong and firm."

Looking away from her husband Usha said softly, "Really, there is no other way. I have thought it out thoroughly."

Shailesh took it for granted that she was talking about Somen. He added with a laughter, "Well, the prologue is over. Now will you tell me your decision? I can swear I will never request you to change it."

Usha sat in silence for about a minute. Then she said, "I was getting along fine in my *dada's* family. I had no particular hardship. I'll go back to them tomorrow."

"Go back to them? When will you return?"

Usha answered, "Please forgive me. I can not come back. I have given much thought to the matter. It is impossible for me to stay here. This is my final decision."

These words turned Shailesh into a stone. All his consciousness hammered this point into his heart that there is no one in this world who can open the iron door that just closed before him.

## *Ten*

After getting up in the morning Shailesh thought he'd had nightmares all night long. Looking through the window he saw Usha was as usual busy with her household work. Somen was with her, perhaps badgering her for food. While climbing down the stairs, when he met Usha, she lifted her face and said, "Your tea is ready. Unless you get ready quickly everything will get cold. So please hurry."

Shailesh replied, "Very well. You can send it, I won't be late even by a minute." So saying it seemed he entered his bathroom galloping all the way. He thought to himself, "What an idiot am I! I took a spat between husband and wife as a solemn declaration of warfare and spent the whole night in unrest and anxiety." Thinking of it he felt not only like laughing but it also made him ashamed of himself. While living together, if a difference in opinion or a tiff would make a wife leave her husband and take shelter with her brother there would be no species called human left in this world. If it was Somen's mother there could have been some concern for a few days. But Usha was a wife made up of ideal Hindu values, which made her to have no other thought but religion and husband. If a few heated words from him would wash away all of her lifelong learning and culture then how could any enduring thing be left in this world? There could be nothing more absurd than worrying about it. Having reached this unquestionable conclusion all apprehension and anxiety left him and peace and joy filled his heart. Comparing Usha with Bibha and a few other educated ladies of his acquaintance he thought to himself that he had enough of them. Should he ever have a daughter he wished her to be like her mother. He would be thankful to God if his daughter would cultivate such values and culture. While having these thoughts he came out of the bathroom in a hurry and entered his study.

Suddenly he felt delighted when the newly appointed Muslim butler came with tea, toast, butter, and cake for his breakfast. He was used to such things all his life except for the few days of interruption recently. When the butler left, after leaving these on the table, he lost his appetite as soon as he looked at them. Since Usha came into his house, instead of this type of breakfast, she herself made *kachuri*[1], *nimki*[2] and such items were served with tea and she would also be present there. Since none of these were there today he didn't feel like eating anything. He poured only a cup of tea from the pot and calling after the butler he sent the rest away with him. Then he anxiously waited to hear a very familiar footstep from outside the curtain. He wasted a lot of time in thinking of giving a tough explanation for not eating his breakfast. When he went back to drinking his tea it was too cold and tasted awful. The butler came back to take the teacup but his eagerly anticipated footstep was not heard. Usha did not come into his room.

Gradually the day was wearing on and it was time for Shailesh to get ready for college after taking bath and meal. As usual Usha sat near him during mealtime. No one in the household noticed any difference in Usha's taking care of her husband or in her conversation. Only Shailesh noticed it. He was dumbfounded to see how far-removed a person could become in only one night, effortlessly and without any fuss.

When he came to his room to change his clothes before going to the college he noticed the small account book on the table. Perhaps it had been lying there since the day before and he hadn't noticed it. Otherwise it was not possible or true that Usha has kept it there for him just now. It was not the last day of the month and why was it needed now? Yet his putting on the tie remained unfinished. Partly for curiosity and partly for absentmindedness he began to turn the pages one by one and he stopped at the last page. The same things were written page after page — same fish, vegetable, bag of rice, salaries paid to servants and so on. Totals of debits and credits till the previous day and the balance in hand was neatly recorded.

---

1 A deep fried snack made with wheat flour.

2 A deep fried salty snack made with wheat flour.

He was in Allahabad when this book was opened. He had no role in it and even if it ends here he would have nothing to do with it. Shailesh stared, unblinkingly, at the first page for a long time. This was only for a few days' matter in running his household. He never had it before and if it did not continue in the future his household wouldn't come to a grinding halt. Perhaps he himself would forget all about it in a few days. Still so many things came to his mind. After closing the book he went back to putting on the tie. All of a sudden it came to him that the value of anything in this world does not remain fixed forever. This seemed to him as the most important thing. There was a day when this notebook and keeping accounts was the most needed thing and now it was on its way to become inconsequential.

At last, after getting dressed he went out. No matter how much he desired, Shailesh could not call Usha and ask her any question. In his heart he was knocking again and again at the door of his unknown future. Yet he could not find in himself the courage to make the uncertain apprehension into a certain disaster.

## *Eleven*

After college Shailesh, instead of coming home went straight to Bibha's. After arriving there he found that his guess was right. His brother-in-law had not gone to the court and meanwhile the two had come to an understanding after their tiff. He felt happy about it. "Bibha, why didn't you send anyone to bring Somen here?" he asked.

Bibha was about to say something when Kshetramohan said, "The one who bought the elephant no longer exists."

"Meaning what?"

Kshetramohan said, "Haven't you heard the story? A man, while he was drunk, wanted to buy the king's elephant. Next day, when he was caught and asked to explain his insolent behavior he, folding his palms, replied that the real buyer of the elephant wasn't there any longer, he had gone away." Then he began to laugh at his own joke. When he stopped laughing he told, "Tell this story to *bouthakrun* and ask her not to be angry. The real buyer is no more. She has fled. If your son is to be raised by his *pishi*, instead of his mother then I would rather somehow borrow the money and buy Bibha an elephant." Giving Bibha a side-glance he began to laugh again.

But Shailesh could not join in that laughter. He was apprehensive of Bibha taking umbrage of the joke and that would refuel her resentment. So he controlled himself with great difficulty and remained silent.

Kshetramohan, feeling embarrassed asked, "What's the matter, Shailesh?"

Shailesh answered, "I was rather worry-free about Somen because of Bibha's assurance. Since that is not going to happen I will have to make some new arrangement."

Kshetramohan commented, "You mean to say that you can't trust that evil witch with your son. Is that it?"

Shailesh said, "Instead of responding to your harsh comment I can only say that Usha will soon be going away."

"Going away? Where?"

Shailesh answered, "From where she came — to her parent's home."

Kshetramohan's visage became very serious. He gave a meaningful eye to his wife and added, "I was afraid of something like this happening."

So long Bibha did not say a word. She understood the meaning of the familiar tone of her husband's comment. But she turned her face away and asked in a normal tone, "*Dada,* are you going to do this arrangement, using me as an excuse? If so, I won't stop you. But I can assure you one day both of you will bitterly regret it."

Shailesh, shaking his head, replied, "No! " Then he narrated the whole sequence of events, starting with the Muslim butler and ending with the morning's account book. He added, "I did not ask her to leave. But I won't stop her either. There will be commotion among our relatives and friends. I know it well that there will be no glory in it for me. But I'll sincerely thank God for amending a serious mistake."

Bibha sat there in silence. Kshetramohan, too, didn't make any comment for a long time. Shailesh broke the silence, "It is my duty to tell you everything. That's why I came here. At least you should not misunderstand me."

Kshetramohan shook his head vigorously. "That is not possible," he said, "That reminds me, Shailesh, has the party in Bhwanipur who was interested in you before contacted you in the meantime?"

Losing his patience Shailesh replied, "Your innuendo is so uncivil and mean it is really impossible not to lose self-control. But you can be forgiven because you don't know where you are striking." Saying which he rearranged his position and sat up straight in his chair.

Kshetramohan looking at his face unfazed and calmly admitted, "You are right. I could not guess your soft spot correctly."

Being piqued Shailesh said, "Having seen the way you treated your wife the other day what else can I expect from you! I never said anything because it would have hurt your pride. Now I think that I should have said it long ago."

Kshetramohan commented with a smirk on his face, "That is right Shailesh. It reminds you of *treating one's wife!* To this day I could not get the hang of it and the time for learning has long passed me by. But you could have written a book about it, brother. Now you two, brother and sister, can discuss the matter without any interference. I'll be back shortly." Abruptly he stood up and walked out briskly.

Calling after him aloud Shailesh said, "It may take me some time to write the book. Meanwhile you should know something about the sarcastic remark you made about Bhwanipur. Should no one from their side contact me I'll have take the initiative to contact them."

Kshetramohan responded from outside the door, "Certainly! Already some valuable time has been wasted."

Next morning Kshetramohan showed up in the Pataldanga house. Shailesh was getting ready for his bath when he was very surprised to see his brother-in-law there. He didn't expect him to come uninvited so soon after the previous day's unpleasant incident. Feeling somewhat abashed he asked, "Is the High Court closed today?"

Kshetramohan replied with laughter, "The question is superfluous."

Shailesh added, "Then have you given up your practice."

Kshetramohan responded, "It is even more superfluous."

Shailesh said, "Perhaps I too am superfluous. It is time for my bath. I don't think you have any objection to that."

Kshetramohan replied, "You may go."

"*Bouthakrun*, can I come in?"

There was no shrine room in the house. Usha was getting ready to sit down in a corner of the bedroom to say her daily prayer to God. Having recognized the voice she drew the edge of her sari over her wet hair and invited him, "Please come in."

Coming into the room Kshetramohan felt embarrassed. He said, "I am imposing myself at this inconvenient time. Did you decide all of a sudden to go to your parent's home? Is your father ill?"

Usha answered, "My father is not alive."

"Oh, is your mother ill?"

Usha replied, "She passed away before my father."

In utter surprise Kshetramohan asked, "Then where are you going? Who do you have there? You can't leave under this circumstance. Not to speak of Shailesh, even we can't agree to it."

Usha, bending her head down a little said with a soft laughter, "Can't you agree?"

"No, under no circumstances!"

"But I have spent so many years with my brother's family, Kshetra Babu. Time didn't stop for me."

Kshetra Babu said, "If you really have to go please tell me truly when you are coming back. Otherwise you can not go!"

Usha was silent. Kshetramohan said, "But what about Somen?"

Usha answered, "His *pishi* is there."

Kshetramohan responded with folded palms, "She is my wife. I am begging your forgiveness on her behalf."

Usha remained silent.

"Can't you forgive her?"

With her head bent down Usha remained seated in silence. Waiting a while for a response Kshetramohan slowly asked with a long and dispirited sigh, "When there are offences in this world, there are punishments too. And it must be that way. But can you tell me why there is no justice?"

Usha said, "You mean why one must suffer for another's offence? I only know that it happens that way at times. But I don't know Kshetramohan Babu why it happens."

"When will you go?"

"As soon as *dada* can come. It may even be tomorrow."

After a moment's silence Kshetramohan Babu said, "I thought I'll never tell you this. But I think I'll be committing an offence if I would keep it a secret. There was the possibility of bringing some one else here before you came. I don't think that the conspiracy is dead."

Usha said, "I know."

Kshetramohan said, "Taking umbrage you will make the conspiracy the winner? Will that—"

He could not finish the sentence. Usha calmly but firmly said, "Let it be the winner or the loser Kshetramohan Babu. But you please do forgive me." So saying, she raised her folded palms to her face while gazing at Kshetramohan's face.

Kshetramohan stood there in silence, looking at that gaze.

## *Twelve*

Shailesh stopped talking to his wife but Usha did not stop talking to her husband. There was not the slightest change in her behavior — she was doing all the housework as always. Shailesh could not bring himself to ask her any questions. His biggest problem was to comprehend how one could have so much loving attachment to the house, which she would be leaving forever. That very morning he had heard Usha scolding a new servant for wiping his hands on a wall. Though she herself, as a force of habit, never makes a mistake in her own work Shailesh could never even find the slightest thing remiss in her sharp watch over everything! He did not have enough time to know Usha very well, in fact he knew very little about her. From the little he knew of her, Shailesh was certain that Usha would be steadfast in her determination to leave. Even then, the incongruity with his accumulated experience with general human nature up to this point in his life was taking his heart through a roller coaster ride with tears in one eye and laughter in the other.

Kshetramohan came to the kitchen door and asked, "*Bouthakrun,* how long do I have to wait for receiving *prasad*?"

Usha drawing the edge of the sari over her head a little more down said with laughter, "You would better ask your most important relative about that. Otherwise I am ready with everything."

Kshetramohan said, "It is not in you to lose. But the loss is mine. Having seen the elaborate cooking *bouthakrun,* I am tempted to eat, even though my stomach is full. But I am afraid of getting sick. However, you can't cancel the invitation for I'll come some other day to enjoy your cooking."

Usha remained silent. Kshetramohan asked, "Where is your son?"

Usha answered, "He had a sudden fancy for not going to school today. I have cajoled him to eat a little and then sent him to school"

Kshetramohan, said, "He loves you very much." Then he added with a smile, "That reminds me, what happened to your idea of your going to your parents' home? Really, *bouthakrun*, how can we depend on anything in this world if you stick to some inappropriate utterance on the spur of the moment."

Usha did not respond to this accusation. With her head bent low she remained silent. Kshetramohan left the place and entered Shailesh's room. Standing in front of a mirror he was combing his hair after he had finished his bath. Turning his face Shailesh looked at him.

Kshetramohan asked, "Is the college closed today?"

"No. But I don't have any class in the first two hours."

Kshetramohan said with a sigh, "But what arrangement have you made for *bouthakrun's* journey to her parents' home?"

Shailesh replied, "Whatever arrangement have to be made I'll do that after her departure. I hear that her *dada* will come tomorrow to take her."

Kshetramohan said, "You are an idiot. You are incompetent to deal with this wife of yours. You would better make a swap. You will be happy and so will I."

Extremely annoyed, Shailesh said, "You are quite advanced in your age. It is high time that you stopped these vulgar jokes."

Kshetramohan said, "It is not for lack of trying that I can't stop. It is your behavior that won't let me stop. Being very much aggrieved she said that she would go to her parents' home and your response was that she could go and you haven't let go of Bhwanipur. What sort of treatment is this? You two, brother and sister, are made from the same mould. Be that as it may, I have undone everything. She is not going anywhere. Don't you again rub her in the wrong way." Suddenly he looked at his watch and exclaimed, "Oh my God, it is getting late for me. I am going now and I'll be back tomorrow morning." As he was leaving he said softly, "Make a little compromise for a few days, Shailesh. She comes from a pundit's family and can not tolerate unholy practices. Why not stop eating food prepared by your butler! Besides these things are not good for your health — at least think of the expenses! I am off now, brother." Saying which, he left in a hurry without waiting for a response.

For a while Shailesh stood there stunned. He had no idea about when Kshetramohan had come, what he said or how he suddenly turned everything upside down.

The orderly came to inform that his food had been served. As usual, in the verandah on the north side, there was a seat for him on the floor and the food was served there. Like everyday, after serving many items for him Usha was sitting nearby. Shailesh, with his head bent low, began to eat. Many times he wanted to verify Kshetra's statement and say sweet-nothing to please Usha. No matter how much he wanted he could not raise his head nor ask about it. At last after finishing his meal he silently got up and left.

## *Thirteen*

Next morning Abinash came. Shailesh had just come out of the bathroom and was going to his study for his tea and breakfast when he got a jolt in his heart at the sight of this unfamiliar face. He politely asked, "Who are you?" The stranger was Usha's younger brother. After introducing himself he said, "*Dada* himself could not come and he has sent me to escort *didi*[1]."

"Very well, you can take her." So saying Shailesh went into his room. Everything for his breakfast was neatly arranged on his table. But pouring only a cup of tea he sat in a recliner. The food remained untouched on the table. He did not have any intention of even touching it. Someone was expected to come from Usha's family to take her. So it was not shocking to see Abinash. At the same time, just because someone had come it was not obligatory for the other one to go. It was also possible that ultimately no one was leaving. There was no way to explain how he felt until something was known with certainty. Kshetramohan was expected to come that morning. Did he forget altogether or did some urgent business hold him up? All of a sudden, these apprehensions became stronger than all others to him. If Kshetramohan was here some resolution was possible. This was what he needed most. In the turmoil of his impatience he was afraid of not being able to control himself and run to Usha and ask her what Kshetramohan had discussed with her the day before. Shailesh felt like he was losing confidence in himself. When he was tired of looking at his watch and the time seemed to be standing still the person who entered the room, parting the heavy curtain, was not the much anticipated Kshetramohan but Abinash. Lifting his face Shailesh gave him a glance and then he picked up a book. Fire seemed to spread all through his body.

---

1 Elder sister, elder female cousins, and other elder women of the same generation and between grandparents and granddaughters.

Abinash was about to sit down when the saw the food. He saw a chair afar and pulling it further away he sat in it. He could not depend on the lord of the manor to welcome him. When he did not even ask the reason for his coming into the room Abinash spoke on his own accord. "*Didi* wants to leave by the two-thirty train," he said.

Raising his head Shailesh said, "Does she? Is she anticipating any kind of resistance from me?"

Abinash was a young boy. Failing to come up with an appropriate answer, he simply said, "No, sir." Having heard the sound of bangles outside the door Shailesh became intransigent. "I have no objection to her going," he said.

Abinash remained silent. Shailesh asked, "Your elder brother was supposed to come. Why didn't he come?" Shrinking into himself Abinash softly said, "He was not that keen to send me either."

"Why?"

Abinash was silent.

Shailesh said, "You are too young and I can't tell you everything. Besides, it is of no use telling you. Yet if your brother ever wants to know tell him that Usha is not at fault in this matter. If it is anyone's fault or mistake it is mine. I should never have sent for her."

Remaining quiet for a moment or two he continued, "I thought that my father had done injustice to her. When the opportunity came after a long time I thought of amending it. Your *didi* came all right. But one mistake mushroomed into a hundred."

It needed no response. Abinash remained silent. Just at that moment, opening the door on the other side Kshetramohan entered. Shailesh looked at him but he could not stop. The nature of harsh words is such that they become harsher by their own weight. Usha was standing behind the curtain. In the frenzy of hurting her more and more Shailesh lost his senses and aiming unmistakably at Usha he continued, "It is true that one day long ago I married your sister, but she is not fit to be called my partner in any manner whatsoever. Our education, culture, standing in society and way of living — nothing is the same. I could insist on keeping her in this house and turn it into a Sanskrit school for Hindu *Smriti scriptures*. But I could never let my only sister, in her shame and sorrow, abandon me and see my only son's head stuffed with bad examples and unhealthy education and training. But I am grateful to her that she has voluntarily done the difficult task of leaving, which I could not ask her to do."

Speechless Kshetramohan gazed at him in awe. By nature Shailesh was shy, mild mannered, and it was against his nature so speak harsh words. But what he did was like a completely deranged man! Kshetramohan had heard that Usha's younger brother had come to escort her. He had no doubt that the young visitor was he. And what was this going on right in his presence? Kshetramohan clasped the young man's two hands in earnest request, "Please never ever tell your sister even one word of it."

The young man, pointing his finger at the door-curtain and nodding his head said, "I don't have to tell her anything, standing outside she heard every word of it."

"Is she standing outside? Over there?"

Before the young man could respond Shailesh said, "Yes, Kshetra, I know that she is standing over there."

After hearing his response Kshetra sat there motionless with an ashen face.

Two or three hours later, when Abinash started for the station, with his sister Somen was in his *pishi's* house, his father was in his college and Kshetramohan was sitting in the library of the High Court.

Next morning, Bibha, sitting at the tea table gave a meaningful glance at her husband and asked, "What did you see *dada* doing?"

Kshetramohan said, "I saw a book in his hand. But in reality he was perhaps doing repentance!"

"When will you do that?"

"Which one? Read a book or repent?"

Bibha responded, "Book will not look good in your hand I was talking abut the latter."

Being needled Kshetramohan said, "If you can send for your brother and live in your parents' home I can begin."

Bibha's mind was contented today. She did not become angry. "I don't think I would be able to do it," she said, "For I did not get the opportunity of learning the art of saying the daily prayers and meditation of the Hindus nor its laws of pollution by touch."

Kshetramohan was getting impatient with his wife's views these days. But he controlled his temper and said in his easy going manner, "It is very unfortunate that you did not get the opportunity. If you had your brother did not have to suffer this misery today." Saying which, he left the room.

## *Fourteen*

Attempts were made again to find a suitable groom for the well educated potential bride in Bhwanipur. This time Bibha could not openly join for the fear of her husband's heartfelt aversion. But she didn't refrain from showing sympathy in many ways from behind the scene. At the request of the bride's side when Kshetramohan bluntly asked Shailesh he denied having any desire and replied in a straight forward manner, "The major part of my life is behind me, Kshetra, and I don't want to get involved in any new encumbrance."

It becomes apparent when a person speaks sincerely. Today Kshetramohan felt pain in his heart. Since that day he began to frequently visit Shailesh on his way back from the court. He had no wife or child in the house and he was getting by with three or four servants. In no time the house became such a disorganized mess that it became a painful sight. After about a month, raising the old issue Kshetramohan said, "You know my views very well. It is difficult to live without a companion. In old age, in particular—"

Uma was present that day. She interjected, "Old age is still far away and *boudi* will come back long before that. How long can one stay in her parents' home out of indignation?" So saying she looked at her brother's face and then at Shailesh's. But none of them answered. Shailesh's face, in particular, suddenly became gloomy. Since Uma continued to stare at his face Shailesh, shaking his head said, "No, she will not come back again."

With the conviction of utter incredulity Uma asserted, "Won't she? Certainly she will come. She can even come back before the end of this month. Can't she, *dada?*"

Her *dada* knew how difficult it would be for her to return. Every word that Shailesh had said just before her leaving was chiseled in her heart. He could not even imagine that Usha would ever be able to forget those words. Shailesh's father had done untold injustice to his daughter-in-law. When she came back Bibha, out of spite, had inflicted many insults on her. But Shailesh, himself, dealt out the ultimate indignity to her the day she left. Yet, considering Usha's upbringing with Hindu scriptural learning and culture, and particularly because of her very sweet nature, Kshetramohan could never approve of her leaving her husband's home for good.

Whenever it pained his heart Kshetramohan used to find consolation in thinking that Usha could endure disrespect and indifference to herself but she could not bear her husband striking at her religious practices. Perhaps it was for this reason that when the call came from her husband's house after a long time she had no hurt feelings, shame and embarrassment. She came without uttering a word or judging anyone.

Kshetramohan, enlightened and free of Hindu sacramental injunctions, was not very much familiar with a Hindu woman's attachment to her religious practices. Comparing the one in his own household with the steadfastness of another's belief and her ability of self-sacrifice he began to think of his own society as small-minded and insignificant. He thought to himself that none of the women in their society had so much strength and spiritedness. He thought it a shame that perhaps this religiosity has been totally banished from their lives.

Did Bibha or Uma have such faith that does not back away from own suffering or do they have that deep respect for their faith which can be tested by the fire of hardship and sacrifice? Could any of the other women he knew be compared? This feeling used to fill his heart with embarrassment on the one hand and deep respect on the other. It was clear to him how much Usha had come to love her husband in such a short time. In the next moment he thought that a Muslim butler was at the center of such a big upheaval, that resumption of the practice, which she did not condone, drove her out of the house forever. Kshetramohan was overwhelmed with awe and resentment, thinking of this inconsequential pettiness of *bouthakrun* in spite of whatever others might have done to her.

After asking the question Uma was gazing at her *dada*. When no answer was forthcoming she asked in surprise, "What happened? *Dada*, you did not answer".

"About what?"

Uma reminded him, "I said that perhaps *boudi* may come back before the end of this month. Don't you think so, *dada*?"

He avoided answering his sister's question. Instead he said, "Let us assume that she is not coming back. She was not here for a long time and she may not be here in the future. Does that mean there is no other way? I was thinking of that."

Uma didn't quite understand and she gazed in silence.

Noticing her surprised look Shailesh said, "Uma, I don't think that her coming back will be appropriate. She is married to me but I can not call her partner or co-practitioner of religion."

Kshetramohan was annoyed at this indecent insinuation about Usha. "If we don't have any religion how can you talk about co-practitioner of religion?"

Shailesh said in utter surprise, "Don't we have any religion?"

Kshetramohan quipped, "Show me where we have it. We make money and have a living. That's all! We can live without a co-practitioner of religion. People of those days gone by had their sacraments and rituals like the *sradh*-peace offering, deity worship rituals, and other religious rituals. They needed a co-practitioner. Why do we need that rigmarole?"

Being cut to he quick Shailesh said, "Is that a co-practitioner? *Sradh*-deity worship- rituals —?"

He could not finish. Kshetramohan interrupted, "It is really that, brother, and nothing else! You are a Hindu and so am I. Don't take offence in my saying that we don't do any worship, don't go to any temple, we don't have the bad habit of bothering deities like Krishna or Vishnu with our supplication. Our women are even more harmless. We are simple folks — decent folks. We have no need for such a five or seven syllable *sahadharmini*[1]. A mono syllabic *stri* is good enough for us. You, brother, please give your consent. The party in Bhwanipur is very much after me and your sister, also, very much wants it to happen. Listen to me, Shailesh."

---

[1] A wife associated with her husband in practice of virtues; simply stated, a wife.

Standing up with a gloomy face Shailesh said, "You are being sarcastic with me."

Seeing the turn of the events Uma got anxious. Being afraid Kshetramohan repeatedly said, "No, brother no! If I have done any such thing I meant it more for me than you."

Shailesh didn't protest. He simply stood there motionless.

## *Fifteen*

Kshetramohan did not muddy the water anymore. Thinking of giving Shaileshwar about a week's time to simmer down his agitation and anger and hoping that, then, one day he would come back to talk about the Bhwanipur matter, he came home with Uma on that day. But before the week could be over, suddenly he had to leave Kolkata in connection with a case in the Chapra court. Before leaving he assured the prospective bride's side and Bibha of the groom's side that the case was not as hopeless as it seemed. On the contrary, the fish was inclined to nibble and he would not be surprised if it suddenly swallowed the hook, line, and sinker.

After a long time he had an amiable discussion with his wife. Bibha had heard some of the developments from Uma. She said, "I thought you were a close friend of your Usha-*boudi.* A month back I could never even think that you could be interested in arranging *dada's* remarriage.

Kshetramohan agreed, "Could I have had such a thought a month back? But now I can not only think of it but also think it to be the right thing to do. Still I am a friend of Usha-*bouthakrun* and I'll always wish her well. It is futile to bang your head against a stone wall for something that can not be and no good will come of it even if it happened."

Bibha, piercing her husband with a wise as an owl smile on her face said, "Because you are men you took so long to figure out *bouthakrun* but I fathomed her on sight. We could have never got along with her."

Kshetramohan said, "I saw that with my own eyes. She had to go away and there is no doubt that we had our differences of opinion about her. There is no use discussing how things could have been under different circumstances. But I agree with you that I made a slight error in judgment."

Bibha replied, "That's enough. I was getting scared the way you were euphoric about praising *jap-tap*[1] and other Hindu practices. We are neither Christians or Muslims; but why is this vanity that everyone is lower than I and my high caste's purity will be polluted with your touch or by eating with you at the same table! The notion that the only right way is the *Bhattachajje*-way and all other roads lead to hell may be tenable in her parents' home but not here. And it is for this very reason that there was no room for her in her husband's house."

This assertion was neither true nor false. Since it was tangled in the web of both truth and falsehood Kshetramohan kept on staring at his wife's face and could not say anything in response.

Just at that moment entering the room Uma asked in utter astonishment, "What's the matter, *dada*?" Continuing with her line of reasoning Bibha added, "Is protecting the sanctity of her caste the most important thing for *boudidi*? Let us assume that you were right in your complaint that *dada* insulted her only because of me, didn't you insult me in the same way taking her side? Is that enough reason for me to leave you and go to my parents' home? Would you suggest that?"

Kshetramohan answered, "No, I don't say that."

Bibha added, "I know you can't say that." Addressing Uma she said, "Your *dada* was dazzled by seeing the exterior appearance of an unexpected object. We were not taught the orthodoxy of Hindutva, but what we got from our parents was more civilized and truthful." She added with a grin, "Your *dada* wanted you to learn many things from his *bouthakrun*. I don't have the time to hear it all now, dear. But why don't you tell your *dada* what you learnt from her and what remained unlearned." So saying she left with a smirk on her face.

Kshetramohan sat there in silence. Her sardonic arrows pierced him deep but he could not give any fitting response. They were far removed from Hindutva but in his imagination he was very much

---

[1] Telling the beads while repeating God's name and meditation.

attracted to observance of codes of conduct by women and the lifestyle of good old days. That was why he was so enchanted by the sudden familiarity with Usha. He felt humiliated before everybody because of her conduct. He had, time and again, proudly espoused to his family and friends the virtues of this ideal housewife's conduct and her sacramental practices. This pride was very much hurt. Only Usha was responsible for herself. Her offence did not touch anyone else and it could never do that. Though he wanted to emphasize this to all, he could not bring himself to say it. So when his wife left he told Uma, by way of an explanation, in a doubtful tone, "I admit that bigotry in anything is bad, Uma. We have to wipe out this blotch from Hinduism. But it would be wrong to deny that we are far worse."

Uma always maintained her silence in all arguments between her *dada* and *boudi*. Even though Bibha was not there she remained silent.

Before leaving for Chapra that night Kshetramohan called Bibha to say, "I will probably return in four or five days. Meanwhile if you happen to meet anyone from Bhwanipur you can tell them that I'll be able to get Shailesh's consent."

Bibha asked, "Then will *bouthakrun* never come back?"

Kshetramohan responded, "No. The more I think about it the more I see that she is guiltier than Shailesh. You have said it right. The teaching that make people so narrow minded and self centered, however good it might have been at one time in the past, has no value in this age. At least we don't need to reintroduce it among ourselves. *Bouthakrun* had only the pretence of scriptural rules and observances but there was no substance in them. If it were not so she would not have abandoned the security of the shelter of her house. Well I am off now," so saying he went out and sat in the car.

It took him ten and not five days to settle the case and return to Kolkata. As he entered the house the first person he met was Uma. She gave the news, "About two days back Shailesh Babu left for Allahabad with six months' leave of absence. Also he withdrew Somen from the school and took him along."

"All of a sudden why has this happened?"

Uma said, "I am not sure. When he came to take Somen he said he was not keeping well."

Entering Bibha's room and addressing her Kshetramohan commented, "It is expected that he would not be in good health but that is no way to cure it." He was going to say more but stopped when he saw Uma was standing there.

## *Sixteen*

Kshetramohan's days passed the same way as it did for other junior barristers. When he would run short of money he would praise Hindutva and its way of living but when some money would come his way he would be quiet and days would pass in the usual way. He was a sincere well wisher of Shailesh. He knew him well and he also knew that an indecisive person like Shailesh could be made to do anything. It was for this conviction that he had not give up his grip on the Bhwanipur party. He used to assure them that the delay was simply for his return from Western India. He still cherished the same affection for *bouthakrun.* His respect for her was also undiminished but there was no need for her return. Wherever she might be may she be in good heath and be safe. Also may her attainment in religious life reach progressively higher heights, but there was no need for her coming into Shaileshwar's household.

Frequently a mistake raised its head in Kshetramohan's mind. It was likely that Usha could not love her husband; perhaps it was not possible for her. Since her childhood she was raised in the environment of orthodox religious practices. So "life after" was more dear to her than "life here and now". So leaving her husband was so easy for her. Kshetramohan, the husband, was as fearful as he was pained at Usha's conduct.

He used to think that she had come to love Somen so quickly because of her strong sense of duty. Since she did not have real affection for him there was no feeling of attachment for him on the day she left for good.

When they were passing their days in Kolkata in this way, the news came from Allahabad after about two months that, at this tender age, Somen was given his *sacred thread* ceremony. His father has also taken initiation from a devoted *Vaishnavite*[1]. The father and son did not miss bathing in the Ganges even for a day and Shailesh never walked through the street where fish or meat was sold.

Having heard the news Uma was laughing up her sleeve. Bibha asked, "Who played the joke? Was it Jogesh Babu?"

Kshetramohan said, "The news came from Jogesh Babu indeed. But their relationship was not light enough for playing this joke!"

Bibha said, "He is *dada's* friend. So what is wrong if he did it?" Stopping for a moment or two she continued, "Do you know why? He had heard all about *boudi* from *dada* and among all the people you were the only one to fall for her orthodoxy — that's why the joke is on you." She continued with laughter, "You won't lose so many cases if you would consult me often before pleading your cases. — Uma, get ready in a hurry. Labanya would be angry if we don't arrive before seven. Advise your *dada* secretly to consult me often. The people who pay him would be happy with the result."

Uma, again laughed up her sleeve. She understood that her *boudi* guessed correctly the reason for Jogesh Babu's playing the joke.

Five or six days later Kshetramohan brought a lengthy letter and dropped it in front of Bibha. "It is written by Jogesh Babu's father — seventy or seventy-two-years-old. I have never laid my eyes on him and I know him through letters only. I don't know what kind of a person he is but he certainly wouldn't play jokes on me."

It was a long letter written in Bengali. Bibha read the letter twice from the beginning to the end and then raising her head asked, "What's the matter? It seems that you will have to go there once."

"But I don't have even a minute's time."

Bibha said, "You can not say that. In this hour of need if we don't stand by them who else will? There is not even a shred of doubt that it is a very serious matter even if half of what is in this letter is true!"

---

[1] A worshipper of Vishnu; (in the context of the story a follower of Chaitanya.

Kshetramohan, nodding his head in agreement, said, "I quite agree with you in this matter. But how can I go? Moreover, even if I went, what is the certainty that this very serious problem will be solved?"

Both of them sat there in silence for a long time. At last, holding back his sigh of despair, Kshetramohan commented, "Everything is possible for Shailesh. He doesn't have even one iota of what you can call determination or strength of mind. Let him go to the dogs. But I feel very sorry that he is leading his son in a wrong path. By whatever means you can you must stop that."

Bibha sat there motionless with a sad and somber face.

She could rain tears, show her hurt feeling, shame and embarrassment and more. But she knew in her heart that she was incapable of stopping it. Kshetramohan, remaining frozen for a while slowly said, "I had doubts all along but now I know for sure that your *dada* really loved Usha. He never loved Somen's mother so much. All these may be repercussions of that."

Bibha was piqued. She said, "Do you think he is doing all these to win her heart? Look, my brother may be weak-kneed but not sleazy. Such a scheme of buffoonery will not come to his mind for anyone."

How much did Bibha know about this matter of repercussion or rebound? Kshetramohan had read these words in books and he also knew very little about it. So in response to her angry comments he kept silent. He was afraid of engaging in polemics when he was ignorant about the subject.

Whatever might be the reaction Bibha won the battle. Her husband, leaving his work unfinished, had to start for Allahabad within a couple of days. After coming back, what he described in detail was as laughable as it was unpleasant. Shailesh stayed close to Jogesh Babu's house. But Kshetramohan could not meet him. He had gone to Brindaban with his fellow fraternity bothers to pay his homage to the lotus feet of his guru. He met Somen. He was wearing the garb of a *Brahmachari*[1] and doing religious practices

---

1 One who has assumed an austere and celibate life for meditation and realization of God.

sanctioned by the scripture. A pious Brahmin from the area was teaching him *Brahmavidya*, the ultimate reality. After narrating all these Kshetramohan said, "The poor child's eyes were brimming over with tears when he saw me. I think the hardship of eating their food pained him the most."

Bibha had a kind of affection for the boy. Though it might not have been intense, she felt hurt to think that the boy was suffering in a place far away from home. Her eyes were flooding with tears. "Why didn't you bring him by force?" she asked.

"It is not that I didn't have the same impulse," Kshetramohan replied. "I thought to myself that the consequence would not be good. I dread sudden passion for religion the most. Shailesh would have been furious with us."

Wiping her tears Bibha said, "Had I known that it had gone so far I would have gone with you."

## *Seventeen*

Though writing letters had almost stopped yet the idiosyncratic deeds of Shailesh did not stop from spreading among his circle of relatives and friends. Perhaps in some quarters the tale had a more colorful appearance. It is needless to say that the news also reached Bhwanipur. It became difficult for Bibha to face anyone. She only bragged to her husband, "Let *dada* return first and then I'll see how he can continue doing it in my presence!"

Kshetramohan would remain silent. He did not believe that Bibha was capable of doing much. But he had confidence in the collective moral pressure of the social circle. Weak-minded Shailesh would not be able to resist that for too long.

Meanwhile Shailesh had extended his leave by four months and only about two months were left of that extension. It was certain that he wouldn't resign from his job. He could bathe in the Ganges in Prayag and tattoo his body with sandalwood paste as much as he wanted. But his fellow brothers of the cult and his guru would never, even at the cost of their lives, give such a disastrous advice as to give up his job. A last attempt would have to be made after his return.

The other day, while drinking tea, Kshetramohan said, "Should Usha *bouthakrun* be here now she wouldn't have to send for her brother in a hurry in order to go to her parent's home. The two would get along fine, doing their *jap-tap* together.

Bibha's face turned gloomy. "Have you heard anything about her coming here?" she asked.

"No."

Bibha remained silent for a moment or two and then suggested, "I have heard that there are black magic and witchcraft in villages. Do you believe that?"

Kshetramohan laughed and said, "No. Even if there is she would not indulge in it."

"Why she wouldn't do it?"

Kshetramohan said, "I am not happy with *bouthakrun.* The respect I had for her has gone. But I can guarantee you that she can't stoop so low."

Bibha did not quite believe him. Slowly she said, "Whatever may happen I give you my solemn promise that I will rescue that boy by force."

The bearer came to tell that Bandhu had come to borrow two pieces of large size carpet. Bandhu was a servant of Shailesh for a long time. Being surprised Bibha asked, "What will he do with carpets?" As they were saying this both of them came outside. Bandhu, saluting them, made the request directly to them.

"Why do you need carpet, Bandhu?"

"I don't know that for sure, m*emsahib,* I think some kind of musical session will take place."

"Who are going to be in it?"

"Two or three people have come with *Sahib.* Most likely they will do."

"Has *dada* returned?"

Kshetramohan asked, "Has Shailesh come?"

Shaking his head Bandhu said, "They all came back last night." After he left with the carpets both of them, heads bent low, remained standing there in silence. Somehow patiently waiting for that day Kshetramohan, accompanied by Bibha and Uma, came to Shailesh's house the next afternoon. They were held back as they tried to enter, by force of habit, the library on the ground floor. The heavy curtain at the door was missing and they could see the inside of the entire room. The appearance of the house had changed radically in a day. The bookcases were there but no other furniture. A white mattress was laid on a blanket on the floor. Seated on the mattress were a couple of barrel-shaped and pot-bellied men, adorned with designs and name of Lord Hari stamped with sandalwood paste all over their bodies and garlands of basil beads hanging from their necks. They panicked to see *sahib* and *mems* there. Without interfering with their leisure the three of them were going upstairs when the cook from Orissa advised them not to go, because the consort of the *Gossain* was there.

"Who is this consort of the *Gossain*?"

The cook from Orissa remained silent.

"Where is *Sahib?*"

In response he pointed his finger towards upstairs. Standing there Kshetramohan began to shout, "Shailesh! Shailesh!" Somen came out running. Seeing his attire and appearance Bibha started to sob out of shock. He was wearing a white piece of cloth without any border, a long tuft of *never cut holy hair* hanging from the top of his head, and a garland of basil beads adorning his neck. He did *pranam* from a distance but did not approach nearer. Uma was going to get hold of him when Kshetramohan signaled her not to do it. "Leave him alone," he said, "Don't touch him so late in the afternoon. They will probably make him to take a bath to purify him. Where is your father, Somen?"

Somen replied, "*Prabhupada,* the guru was reciting the Bhagabad." Kshetramohan said, "Inform his holiness, your father that we are standing here."

"He has been informed and he is coming."

In a few moments Shailesh came down. He was wearing white *dhoti*, without any border, a tunic, and a thin holy tuft of hair was hanging from the top of his head. There was no other change in his outward appearance. But his profound change within could not escape even a moment's glance. His demeanor was very humble and he spoke very softly. When Uma and Bibha did *pranam* he did not come close to touch them but blessed them from a distance.

Kshetramohan said, "Didn't you keep any room in the house for people to sit?"

Embarrassed Shailesh answered, "The outer room is very dirty. It will have to be cleaned."

Kshetramohan said, "Then we bid you good bye now." Addressing Somen he added, "We are leaving now. It looks as if we won't be needed here any more. Yet let me tell you that should there be some arrangement for people to sit please let us know, dear. Now come along."

Shailesh stood there in silence.

Bibha did not say a word to anyone in the car all through the drive home. Only tears rained from her eyes. They understood one thing loud and clear — there would be no room for them in that house anymore. Whatever her *dada* might have done Bibha had made a solemn promise to her husband that she would rescue Somen by force. Both the husband and wife many times remembered those words uttered from the vanity of affection. But none of them could mention it in utter shame.

Over a month had passed after that. Meanwhile, the whole affair had created such a vortex of gossip among friends and relatives that people were not satisfied with the truth. Going from mouth to mouth with embellishments and fabrication the whole affair became so vulgar that it became impossible for Bibha to have any social interaction. Yet there was no way out visible anywhere. Kshetramohan knew that many exciting things in this world subside with time and the only way was to wait patiently. The business of people's overwhelming desire for a better afterlife, once started is very difficult to stop. In the midst of all the uncertainties in life men are driven mad with the hope of certitude of a better afterlife. Along with this was the frightful threat of Usha. She was the one who, both as a friend and an enemy, had laid the foundation of this disastrous affair. Getting even a whisper of it should she appear on the scene there would be no escape from a calamitous ending. At the mere mention of her name not only Uma and Bibha but Kshetramohan also became furious these days. If truth be known this would never have happened if she had not been brought into the house in the fist place.

One Sunday morning both the husband and wife were discussing this matter. Since the day they had to come back from Shailesh's house bearing the burden of insults they never took even one step in that direction. But they were getting all the information none the less. The band of fellow brothers of the cult was not even thinking of moving out. The guru and his consort were installed in the upstairs' rooms as before. Chanting the name of the Lord with musical accompaniment went on unabated every morning and evening. The grandeur of the feast for the Lord was increasing with time. All this news came to Bibha regularly. Only one new thing had been added. It was heard that Shailesh was determined to build an *Ashram* for his guru in the holy city of Nabadwip and he was going around to borrow money for that purpose.

Wan-faced Bibha said, "Should this be true, won't you even try to save *dada*? Will the boy's future be washed out right before our eyes?"

Kshetramohan said with a sigh, "Tell me what can I do?"

Bibha was silent. How she would know what could be done under what circumstances!

Suddenly Kshetramohan said, "Since that day we have never been there, let us go today."

Bibha was crying in her heart. So there was no room for shame or embarrassment in her. She readily agreed. "Let's go," she said.

This time they didn't take Uma with them. They didn't want to increase the burden of their shame in the presence of this young woman. When the car stopped in front of Shailesh's house it was past ten o'clock. The outer room was open. The two fellow brothers of the cult were packing their bundles of possession.

Kshetramohan asked, "Is Shailesh Babu home?"

They looked, lifting their faces up. After keeping silently thinking for a moment or two they answered, "He went to the holy city of Nabadwip day before yesterday."

"When will he be back?"

"May be tomorrow morning or the day after."

"Is Babu's son in?"

Both of them nodded and at once began to mind their packing.

Then after entering the house both of them noticed at the same time that the heavy curtain on the library room door was hanging in its place today. Parting the curtain a little they found that the old furniture was in their usual places. Bibha said, "*Dada* has brought the room back to its original look by just removing those two men. I never hoped that he would ever have the good sense to do this little thing." Before she could finish her say, on hearing a sound, all of a sudden both of them turned their faces and they became speechless. Somen had gone somewhere outside. He was coming back juggling a rubber ball in his hand. His basil bead garland round his neck, the holy tuft of hair on his head and his garb of a *Brahmachari* had all vanished. His body was bare, waist up, but he was wearing a *dhoti* with a beautiful golden border, his hair was well groomed and cut in the normal fashion of Bengali boys and he was wearing a pair of polished pumps. He came running and while hugging Bibha he said, "Ma has come, *pishima.* She is cooking in the kitchen, come on." He began tugging her.

Bibha was thunderstruck. Kshetramohan said, "Your Ma has come, isn't that right Somen? That is why—"

"She came yesterday at noon. Please come, *pishemashay,* come to the kitchen."

"Let's go."

As soon as the three came at the kitchen door, Usha, hearing the sound, washed her hand and came out. Bibha, taking her shoes off, did *pranam* to her. "Did you see *boudi*, what antics happened?"

Usha, touching her chin with her hand kissed it. "I saw it alright, dear," she said while laughing. Looking at the appearance of my son I couldn't stop sobbing. I tore off the garland round his neck as fast as I could and called in the barber to give him a fine haircut. I got him new clothes and shoes. Only after putting on all these on him I could look at him. Well, can you please tell me what you were doing?" She gave a side-glance at Kshetramohan.

Kshetramohan responded, "There is no hurry for it, *bouthakrun,* I'll tell you everything slowly. Let us go upstairs now and have something to eat. Bye the bye, we saw the two fellow brothers of the cult packing their bundles. What did you do with the pair of the guru and his consort? They are not upstairs, I hope!"

Usha said with a laughter, "No, don't fear. They have gone to holy Nabadwip."

"I hope they are not coming back."

Usha, smiling softly, said, "No!"

Kshetramohan said, "*Bouthakrun*, it was beyond my wildest dreams that you would have the good sense to tear off the basil bead garland of a *brahmachari*-brahmin's son with your own hand and shear his *holy tuft of hair* — please tell me, how could this happen?"

Usha, smilingly, repeated Kshetramohan's own words, "Very well, *Jamai Babu,* what is the hurry? Now please come upstairs and let me offer you something to eat."

# Pointing the Path

(*Patha Nirdesh*)

There is a rich boy – poor girl plotline in *Pointing the Path* (Patha nirdesh). Both Guni and Hem fall in love soon after they meet. But their marriage is deemed out of the question by Hem's mother because the rich boy Guni is a *Brahmo* and the poor girl, Hem, is a Hindu. Hem is given in marriage but becomes a widow within a year. The mother is remorseful and dies in grief. Hem is tradition bound but paradoxically empowered by her learning. Guni loves her dearly but can't cross the invisible barrier of Hindu widowhood. Saratchandra firmly maintains the balance between romance and tradition without any fairy tale ending.

## *One*

When the breadwinner of a lower middle class family dies in tuberculosis he also leaves behind a family that is half-dead. Sulochana's husband, Patitpaban, did exactly that. After suffering from the disease for over a year he died in the dead of a blustery monsoon night. Sulochana had gotten the last sacrament of penance administered to her husband the day before and since then she had kept vigil by his bedside without ever moving. Life left her husband silently. Likewise, Sulochana sat in her place in silence, without disturbing the peace of the neighborhood with loud wailing. Her thirteen-year-old unmarried daughter, Hemnalini, had fallen asleep on a mat a little while back. She didn't even wake her up. She continued to sleep without even knowing that her father had breathed his last. There was no servant or maid in the house nor was there even a distant relative. The people in the neighborhood were gradually getting tired of doing their neighborly duties of helping. Moreover, since the afternoon the rain was pouring hard and mercifully no one came that night to sleep on the pretext of watching the dying.

Outside, the deluge continued unabated. Inside, staring at her dead husband, Sulochana sat motionless like a log. Next day after hearing the news everyone came. The men carried the dead body to the cremation ground. The women began to sob and sprinkle the place with cow dung and water.

The only asset Sulochana had was a small grove of mango and jackfruit. With the help of her neighbors she sold it for one hundred rupees to perform the last sacrament for the dead and then she sat in the hut stoically. "What are we going to do now, Ma?" asked the daughter.

"Don't be afraid, dear! There is God," answered Ma.

The money left over after paying for the last sacrament saw them through for a month. Then after finding the sky free of clouds and locking the hut Sulochana stood on the road with her daughter before daybreak.

"Where will you go, Ma?" asked the daughter.

"Kolkata, to your *dada's*[1] home," responded Ma.

"Who could be this brother? You never talked about him!"

After a moment or two of silence the mother added, "I never thought of him until just now, dear."

Hem was a very intelligent girl. Taken aback she stopped in her tracks. "There is no need for going to anybody's home. There may be hardship but we'll scrape along if we stayed on our land. I won't go anywhere leaving our home," she insisted.

Anxiously Sulochana said, "Don't stop Hem. It will soon be dawn."

As they walked she said, "Your father taught you many things. Don't waste it all. You don't have to tell me Hem I know it too that we two will somehow scrape along if we stayed here. But can you tell me dear how am I going to give you away in marriage?"

Hem responded, "You don't have to give me away in marriage."

"If I don't we will be outcasts!"

Hem said, "Let it be, Ma. We two, mother and daughter, will suffer and scrape along together. What would it matter to us if we are outcast or not. There are many other kinds of people in this world who do not make others outcast because they can't marry off their daughters. We would live like one of them."

In spite of her burden of grief Sulochana smiled a little to hear her daughter speak. "Still, we have to leave this village. Once we are made outcasts we'll become pariahs and no one will call us even for menial work like sweeping their courtyard."

---

[1] Elder brother or cousin. It is extended to other elder men out of affection or courtesy. It is also an affectionate term for addressing grandfather or a grandfather-like figure.

Hem gave no response. Many unpleasant memories came to her mind. Suppressing them, she began to walk along the road in silence.

They were walking on the road that ran along the Ganges and then, winding through villages, came to the Sreerampur Railway Station. After walking for about two miles they stopped at the Shiddheshwari temple on the roadside. Drawing the edge of her sari round her neck Hem did *pranam*[1] to the deity and said, "Ma, it is morning now. I am feeling embarrassed to walk on this road now."

Sulochana, herself, was also feeling embarrassed. On seeing an elderly lady on her way to morning ablution she asked, "Ma, isn't this the road to the Sreerampur Station?"

Looking at her face for a moment or two she asked, "From where are you coming, dear?"

Without answering the question Sulochana asked, "Isn't there any other way to the station, Ma?"

A narrow lane, starting from across the temple went all the way to the station. Pointing at that road the old lady said, "This lane goes by the Brahmins' neighborhood and joins the railroad track. Go on this road and after walking along the railroad track turn left to reach the Sreerampur Station. You can go, dear. Don't be afraid, for no one will say anything to you."

Without any hesitation Sulochana, taking her daughter by the hand, entered the lane.

---

[1] An act of veneration (by a Hindu) in which a younger person touches the feet of an elder in order to be blessed by the propitious dust. Also, sometimes the simple act of folding one's palms before another person or a deity.

## *Two*

Gunendra's palatial house on Amherst Street was lying almost vacant. He slept in one room on the third floor and used another room as his study. The other rooms on the third floor and the entire second floor were lying vacant. On the ground floor a cook, two servants and a gatekeeper occupied one room each. The rest of the rooms were all locked up.

Gunendra's father had made so much money in the iron trade, and had accumulated so much wealth at the time of his death that even if he had ten sons instead of just one, none of them would need to earn a penny to live comfortably. Gunendra had deposited in the bank all that money along with the proceeds from the sale of his father's iron business and he was now practicing law without a care in the world.

It was about ten o'clock in the morning and he was still reading a book when a servant came to tell him, "Babu[1], it is now time for your bath,"

"I am on my way," he said. But he continued with his reading just the same.

The servant returned in a few minutes and announced, "Two ladies want to meet you."

Taken aback, he lifted his face from the book and asked, "With me?"

"Yes, Babu, with you. Your —"

---

1 A term of respect attached to a name, like Master or Mr. Instead of addressing a Bengali gentleman as Mr. X (the surname) it is a common practice to address as X-babu (where x is the first name). In the days of the East India Company the clerks in offices were called Babu by the British and even today a supervisory clerk is called Baro-babu. Baro meaning the big(boss).

Before he could finish his say Sulochana entered the room. Gunendra, closing his book, stood up.

Addressing the servant Sulochana said. "You may go back to your work now."

After the servant left the room she asked, "Guni, where is your father, dear?"

Surprised, Gunendra kept on staring at her without saying a word.

Smiling a little Sulochana said, "Looking at my face you can not recognize me, dear. About twelve years ago we used to live in the house next to yours. That year you had your *sacred thread ceremony* and we left for the village that same year. Has your father gone to the shop?"

Gunendra replied, "No, he passed away about three years ago."

"Passed away! And your *pishima*[1]?"

"She too is no more. She left before my father."

Sulochana, releasing a deep sigh, said, "I see that only I am alive. You were only seven years old when you lost your mother. I raised you from then to the time of your *sacred thread ceremony*. Oh, Guni, can't you remember your mother's best friend?"

At once Gunendra bowed down all the way to her feet and taking a few grains of dust from her feet, he stood up, "Yes, Ma! Are you indeed she?"

Sulochana, touching his chin with her fingers and kissing them said. "Yes, my dear. I am she!"

Gunendra pulled a low level stool near her and said, "Please be seated, Ma."

Laughing, Sulochana said, "Since I've come to seek your protection what else could there be for me but to sit! Haven't you gotten married yet, dear?"

It was Gunendra's turn to respond with laughter. "I haven't yet found the time for it."

---

[1] A sister or a cousin sister of one's father, an aunt.

Sulochana responded, "Now it will happen. Isn't there any woman in the house?"

"No."

"Then who does the cooking?"

"There is a Brahmin cook."

"There will be no need for a cook. I'll do the cooking from now on. Well we can discuss that later. I have few other things to tell you. Let me do that first. When my husband lost his job here we went to his ancestral home. We had some cash in hand and there was some land too. We had a more or less comfortable living. Then last year he came down with tuberculosis. He passed away about a month back after making us pauper with the cost of his treatment and change of air. Now my plea to you is that you would provide for this helpless one."

Tears began to rain from her eyes. Gunendra's eyes were also brimming over with tears. Feeling distressed he said, "Ma, have you come here with this apprehension in your mind that a human being might not provide for his mother?"

Sulochana, wiping her tears with the edge of her sari, said, "No dear. I didn't come here with that kind of thought in my mind. If it were so, I probably wouldn't have come here in spite of my utterly distressed condition. You were a little boy when I left. When I thought of you after twelve years in this hour of my depravation I came without any hesitation. Besides, I have one more thing to say to you. My daughter, Hemnalini, who is like a sister to you, is in more dire straits than I. She is old enough to be given away in marriage. But I haven't been able to arrange it. You will also have to do that."

Gunendra asked, "Ma, why didn't you bring her with you?"

Sulochana responded, "I have brought her. She easily feels hurt, abashed and embarrassed. I didn't want her to hear me speak of her plight. So I asked her to wait on the ground floor and I came here alone."

Feeling concerned Gunendra called out for the servant, "Nanda, Hem is waiting downstairs, go and bring her here right away."

Sulochana continued, "It will cost you money to give her away in marriage. That debt I will never—"

Interrupting her Gunendra quickly asserted, "In that case, I would better leave the room and you can say whatever comes to your mind. But I can assure you that if I start talking about my debt to you for what you did for me after my mother's death you too will have to leave the room in embarrassment. I don't see any need for it. You stop talking about it and so will I."

Laughing, Sulochana said, "That is better! But the girl will soon be here and I won't be able to say this to her face. So let me tell it now. But don't you think, Guni, that I am saying so because I see her with a mother's eyes. When Hem will come here you will see for yourself that your sister will not be an unsuitable match for any man either in her beauty or in her qualities. Her father taught her many things. He spent his last few years doing only that. I can say that she would be a treasure to any family she might go into. Hem, come here, dear. This is your Guni dada, do *pranam* to him."

Entering the room Hem, prostrating before Gunendra, stood there with her head bent down. Looking at her weary and wan face from the long journey on foot Gunendra stood there astounded and at a loss to say anything. Perhaps Sulochana could read his thoughts when she said, "Guni, I would have given her into your good hands if our customs and practices did not prohibit it. After my death, Hem will observe ten days of personal impurity and you will observe it for three days. So, according to the codes of right conduct, she is your sister."

Gunendra, pulling himself together, said, "Hem, did you hear that we both have the same Ma. So in mother's home you and I are equals. Come along, let me arrange something for you to eat."

Suddenly Sulochana said, "Guni, why are you not wearing the *sacred thread*?"

Gunendra was bare, waist up. Giving a glance at his neck he said, "We are *Brahmo*[1]."

"*Brahmo*! Oh dear, that was not the right thing to do. Since it has been done, you can do penance for it and then wear the *sacred thread* again."

Gunendra said, "Though it was not my doing, Ma, my father had done it. But I don't see the need for any penance. I do not consider *Brahmo*-religion a bad one."

Sulochana felt like a thunderbolt had struck her heart and she sat down. After a moment or two, releasing a dispirited sigh, she commented, "I don't know why some people engage in such follies."

Smiling, Gunendra said, "We can talk about follies some other time, Ma. Now let us go to the kitchen."

---

[1] One belonging to the Hindu monotheistic reform movement started by Raja Ram Mohun Roy.

## *Three*

A wayfarer, after eating from a clay pot and tossing it out on the wayside, walks away without even giving it a second look to see whether the pot is intact or broken. Likewise, ninety percent of people, after getting what they want from *Saraswati*[1], the goddess of learning, unceremoniously dump her by the highway of *Lakshmi*[2], the goddess of wealth, without giving a second look as to whether she is in one piece or broken into hundred. Gunendra was not of this type. As always, he served *Saraswati* with deep respect and devotion even after becoming a lawyer. His study was becoming filled with books. Hemnalini found a much-welcomed refuge there. Gunendra was not a very well organized person. So when a book came out of a bookcase it didn't easily get back in. After residing on a table or a chair for a while and ultimately on the carpet if it ever got into a bookcase with Nanda's help, it blended so well with the rest that it would not come out when needed. There was a catalogue of books but there was no way of using it.

Within a few days Hem got this chaos well under control and organized. One day, just when she got all the books out of one of the bookcases and emptied it completely Gunendra entered the room. Noticing him Hem said, "Guni da, it would be more convenient if these books were in that bookcase and the books from that one were in this bookcase."

Scrutinizing the situation, Gunendra asked, "What sort of convenience?"

Hem responded, "Well can't you see the convenience? Can't you see if those books were in this bookcase —"

---

[1] The goddess of learning.
[2] The goddess of wealth.

Gunendra said in a somber tone, "I can see it all right. It would be very convenient."

Hem sat down on a low stool and said, "Leave me alone, I won't do it anymore. It is futile to try to do good to you."

Gunendra, picking up a book, went out with a smile.

Since Hemnalini stayed in this room all day and night Gunendra studied in his bedroom. On one Sunday noon Hem called out from outside the door, "Guni da, can I come in?"

From inside the room Guni responded, "Please do."

As she entered the room Hem asked, "Why do you study in your bedroom all the time?"

"What's wrong with that? Would I learn any less in this room?"

"Were you not learning enough in your study all this time?"

Gunendra commented, "Not that I was learning any less but the materials were not well digested. I am assimilating them better in this room."

Hem started to laugh. But since she did not understand the comment well she became somber. "You are always poking fun! Can't you say anything in a straightforward manner?"

Without giving any answer Guni continued to laugh in silence.

Hem said, "But I know why! You don't go into that room because I am there. Do you feel shy around me? I don't feel that way about you at all."

Guni asked, "Why don't you? You should."

Hem, moving a lock of hair from her forehead to her back commented, "Why should I be abashed about you? Are you a stranger? It can't be that way Guni da. Please come to your study." Saying which she picked up the books and went out.

Guni bought some jewelry, such as bangles, bracelets and chains for Hem's everyday use. Having seen them Sulochana commented, "Why did you get all these, dear?"

Guni replied, "Only these few are not enough, Ma. We will need lot more. You can't give your daughter away in marriage without jewelry!"

Sulochana could not say anything else. She was becoming very much concerned in her heart. At all times she pondered how so soon these two could become so close. One day she called Guni to say, "We can't let the coming month of *Agrahayana*[1] pass us by. Somehow she will have to be married off by then. She is becoming quite grown up."

Guni replied, "Don't you worry about that, Ma. But at the same time we can't throw her into hot water either. We must find a worthy bridegroom."

With a long and dispirited sigh Sulochana said, "Worthy or unworthy will be determined by her fate, Guni. We have to do our duty and the rest is in God's hands."

Guni said, "You said it right, Ma." He left with a dark shadow floating over his face. Noticing that, Sulochana released another long and dispirited sigh. She thought to herself, "Things don't look good to me. She must be given away in marriage at all costs."

A few days later entering the room, all of a sudden, Hem said, "You are still lying down and haven't changed yet? Come on, get up quick."

Lying on his bed Guni stared in silence. Hem walked to the cupboard drawer, unlocked it and, taking a bundle of rupee notes in her hand, tied them in a knot to the end of her sari. After locking the cupboard drawer she said, "I beseech you, Guni da, don't waste any more time, please get up. The shops will close soon."

Guni had guessed somewhat from the way she was dressed up. But he asked, "Where do we have to go?"

Getting impatient Hem retorted, "About an hour ago I asked them to get the carriage ready and now you are asking where do we have to go!"

---

[1] The eighth month of the Bengali calendar and the second autumn month, from mid-November to mid-December.

Guni quipped, 'The coachman might know where we have to go. But I am no coachman and how should I know."

Hem laughed. "Why should you be a coachman, Guni da? Let's go. The shop will be closed."

"Which shop."

"It is the bookstore, silly! Didn't Manada tell you earlier? I sent her to inform you. Many good books have come out. I have made a list."

Noticing a piece of paper in her hand he said, "Let me see the list."

"No, then you won't let me buy them."

"Then even if you buy them without my knowledge I won't allow you to read them."

Hem, remaining silent for a moment or two, said, "Very well I'll show it to you in the carriage."

They came back in the evening after buying a carriage-load of books. Seeing them, Sulochana commented, "Good heavens, what will you do with so many books."

Guni commented, "How should I know Ma? They are all Hem's books. She wasted a lot of money, purchasing a lot of useless books."

Sulochana said, "Why did you give her the money?"

Guni replied, "I didn't give her. She had the key, she took the money, she had ordered the carriage ready and then she herself purchased the books. I only went along with her, and nothing else."

Hem had the load of books carried to the third floor — some by Nanda, some by Manada and the rest by her.

Sulochana said, "Guni, don't pamper her so much. God knows where she will land and then she will die in endless sorrow."

Coming to his study upstairs Guni found that Hem, sitting under the gaslight, was attaching number-stickers with glue behind the new books. "Ma was asking me not to pamper you anymore," he said, "You may land in a poor household and will die in endless sorrow."

Piqued, Hem replied, "Why should I die? If I am given in marriage to a poor household I'll come back, running away, the very next day."

Laughing, Guni said, "That would be good!"

Hem didn't say anything in response. Gunendra looked at her in silence and then, holding back a tiny sigh, went back to his room.

*Durga Puja*[1] was over. On the day of *Vijoya* Hem went by carriage to watch the immersion of the images of the goddess. After returning home and doing *pranam* to her mother she went upstairs. Gunendra was walking, back and forth, in the moonlight on the open roof of the third floor. Hem stood before him, bending down and touching his feet with her head to do *pranam* she stood up. Seeing Gunendra staring at her face in silence she seemed to feel abashed for a moment. She said immediately, "Didn't you bless me, Guni da?"

Gunendra came out of his stupor. "Of course I did," he quickly added.

"When did you do that?"

"I did it in my thoughts."

Holding back her laughter, "Tell me what blessing you gave me."

Feeling himself hemmed in and putting on a somber mask he said at last, "It is not appropriate to divulge a blessing. Then it does not come true."

Hem said, "We'll see about that later. Did you do *pranam* to Ma?"

"I do that everyday."

Hastily Hem said, "No, no! That won't do. Today is *Vijoya.* You have to do a special *pranam* today. Please go quickly, otherwise she might feel offended."

---

[1] Worship of the Supreme Mother Goddess, mostly by the Bengalis, in the autumn.

One day, early in November, Hem stormed into the room and immediately said, "Don't you have anything else to think or do? What have I done to you?" So saying she began to sob copiously.

Perplexed, Gunendra asked, "What's the matter, Hem?"

Sobbing Hem, mimicking him said, "As if he doesn't know a thing! 'What's the matter, Hem!' Ma was saying that everything has been arranged in Shantipur or some such place! If I don't want to get married can you make me do it under duress?"

Having found out the reason Gunendra said with a smile, "Oh, that's what it is! You are advancing in age and don't we have to arrange for your marriage?"

"No!"

"How can you say, 'No?' Don't you know that you will become an outcast if you are not married?"

"Do you become an outcast if you are not married?"

Gunendra said, "We can't be outcast for we are *Brahmo.* But you will become a pariah if you are not married at the prescribed age. So we'll have to arrange it."

Wiping her eyes Hem said, "You people are right. You have humanism and that is why you do not sacrifice a human being on the altar of some dead rule. Whatever may be your design I'll never leave this house."

To placate her Gunendra softly said, "The prospective groom also has a large house. He has good reputation. He is learned, wise and wealthy. You will have not a trace of hardship there."

Hem was not mollified in the slightest. Shoving the locks of hair away from her face in a fury she asserted, "I am telling you that will happen under no circumstances. If I have become a burden, you don't have to feed me. I will go without food and stay in my study room. I won't ask for anything."

Forcing a smile on his face Gunendra said, "You will also have a study room there. Should you not have it I will take your room from here and install it there."

Paying no heed to him, with tears raining from her eyes, Hem said, "You don't have to do a thing Guni da, not a thing. In this month of *Agrahayana*? In one month? I beseech you Guni da, you completely undo this arrangement."

Seeing her sobbing copiously Gunendra's eyes were also brimming over with tears. Controlling himself with much effort he said, "How can that be, dear one? All arrangements have been finalized."

"Your arrangement is rubbish. Your finalization is meaningless. You have made this arrangement and you can undo it if you want to. I beseech you, Guni da, with my folded palms, please listen to this plea of mine."

Sulochana, with a suspicious mind, had followed Hem upstairs. Entering the room she said angrily, "What are you doing Hem? What insanity are you talking? Negotiated arrangements regarding marriage can not be undone. Nor can the word of honor, once given, be altered. And why should I undo everything? It is your good fortune that you have such a brother. Such a good match has been found! And you are asking to dissolve the marriage proposal! You are a Bengali girl. Do you wish to live like an old Christian spinster? Go downstairs at once."

Hem went away. Addressing Gunendra Sulochana remarked, "This is the consequence of reading books all day and night. Such evil-minded thoughts come from being immersed in novels and dramas for twenty-four hours. We must send her away for good in this *Agrahayana* by hook or by crook."

Gunendra sat there in silence. Sulochana remained standing there for a while and then she slowly went downstairs.

A couple of days later, after returning from the law court, Gunendra was about to enter the study to fetch a book when Hem called out from inside, "Don't enter, Guni da. I am eating."

Guni stopped dead in his tracks. "You may be eating but will your food be polluted if I merely enter the room?" he asked.

Hem answered, "Don't you see that the floor has wall to wall carpet?"

Guni said, "You don't become an outcast if your maid, Manada, enters your room. Am I lower than even her?"

Embarrassed, Hem said with a smile, "Very well, you may come in. I have finished eating." So saying she pushed the platter of food to the other side of the table.

"No, no, you continue with your eating. You must eat. Let me go and change out of my office clothes." After saying this Guni left in a hurry. He felt like his heart was on fire.

Next morning at about ten o'clock as soon as Guni left his seat after eating his meal Hem rushed in from somewhere and sat down on Guni's seat and asked, "*Bamunthakur*[1], give me food to eat on this platter."

The astounded Brahmin cook said, "Babu has just eaten from that platter!"

Hem responded, "Yes, yes, I know. Why don't you serve me some food?"

On hearing this from the next room Sulochana came near to her and asked, "What are you doing Hem? The platter has been polluted by Guni eating from it. Go and change your clothes and purify yourself with water from the holy Ganges."

Hem took a mouth-full of left over food from the platter and said, "*Thakur*, give me more food. How many people in this world are fortunate enough to eat from the platter from which Guni da has eaten? It is a good fortune indeed to eat from this platter."

Dumbfounded Sulochana looked on as the Brahmin cook served rice, vegetable and other dishes on the platter.

Guni was washing his mouth on the other side of the verandah and he heard every word. He commented in the evening, "It seems Hem has become an outcast today."

Hem was engrossed in reading one of the new books. She replied without lifting her head, "Who told you that?"

"Whoever it may be. Haven't you become an outcast?"

---

1 A cook belonging to the Brahmin caste.

Lifting up her head Hem said, "No! One doesn't become an outcast for eating leftovers from your platter — not even those who invented the caste system."

Sitting down in a chair, not far away, Guni said, "It may be so. But you haven't acted in a proper manner. One should abide by the rules of her caste. Besides it causes heartache to your mother!"

After remaining silent for a moment or two, piqued Hem suddenly said, "As if it is not your home, it is not your property! Your position is below everyone else, and you are the least important! You may tolerate this attitude but I can not. Should I eat your leftovers Ma will be hurt but it will be an affront to the One much more venerable than Ma if I were not to do it. Very well, will you please leave now? I don't feel like talking anymore." So saying she buried her face at once in the opened book.

Gunendra sat there motionless for a while and then he left silently. Suddenly a dusky curtain vanished somewhere from both his eyes.

## *Four*

Towards the end of the month *Agrahayana* Hem was married to someone in a wealthy family in Navadwip. After doing *pranam* from a distance to her Guni da Hem left for her husband's home. She had no father-in-law, mother-in-law or any sister-in-law there. There were only her husband's old grandmother from his father's side and her husband's younger brother who was living in Kolkata and studying there in a college.

Kishoribabu was about thirty-six-years-old. After becoming a widower he was looking for a grown-up bride. So he chose Hem without even seeing her. After his marriage he began to entreat Sulochana to live with them in Navadwip. Consenting to the proposal Sulochana sent a letter to her daughter and adding that she wished to earn merit by living in holy Navadwip.

In her response Hem wrote, "All the people of Navadwip would be redeemed from their sins if they could only have a whiff of the air of the home you are living in now. If you are not earning any merit by living there you won't earn it in heaven itself. Should you come here, abandoning him there, I'll myself go there to live with him."

She knew her daughter too well. Though she could not go, her heart began to roam, all day and night, around a place, called Navadwip, which was quite unknown to her.

Six months passed in this manner. Then she could not control herself any longer. One day, using the pretext of a holy festival, she, accompanied by Nanda, sailed for Navadwip in a steamboat. Having reached there and finding her daughter quite lean and thin she opined sadly, "I suppose that there is no one here to take care of you, dear."

In response the daughter didn't say either "yes" or "no".

The festival was over. When her mother showed no sign of leaving, Hem said one day, "How long are you going to stay in your son-in-law's home Ma? People would speak ill of you!"

Sulochana retorted angrily, "You want to be relieved by getting rid of me! This is at least my own daughter and her husband's home. Who is there to call my own that I should return to "my home"?"

Astounded, Hem sat there for a while and then she responded, "You are not to be blamed Ma. It is our innate nature as women to forget in a day who is our own or another's."

Time marched along and it was the time for *Durga Puja* again. Guni had sent many gifts for the occasion. Calling Hem aside, Sulochana commented, "Though my Guni is *Brahmo* he knows all these Hindu customs."

Distributing the confectioneries to the neighbors' homes and showing off the expensive clothing to them, Sulochana proudly declared to all that even though she was not home her son had sent all these gifts for his sister. She further added that she would return home when the *Puja* was over. Hem had never raised the issue of her returning home after the first time she had done so long go and she made no comments this time too. Reading her daughter's mind, Sulochana thought to herself, "God willing, my dear, one day you will know how much it hurts a mother to be away from her child!"

But Sulochana was struck down with a severe case of malaria before the *Puja* festivities were over. After a month of her suffering from the fever Hem said, "Ma, enough is enough! When in dire straits one has to seek the help of the savior, *Madhusudana*. If you want to live you must send for Guni da." As she was saying this, her eyes were brimming over with tears and then it began to pour. Facing the sky she sat there motionless.

Ma said, "Please do that, Hem. Write him a letter."

Hem wrote a letter to Gunendra to take her mother home and sent it through the manager of the household.

Manada and the gatekeeper arrived two days later. Hem, calling Manada aside, asked, "Why didn't Guni da himself come?"

Manada responded, "He too is sick. He has been suffering from a cough and cold along with fever at times for over two weeks. Otherwise he himself would have come." Hem had hoped that Guni da would come.

Sulochana left. Guni arranged for her treatment and sent her away to the West for a change of air. Maids, servants and all medicines went with her. Before leaving, Sulochana said, "Guni, you are also not in good health. Come with me and let us go together." Guni could not agree to that. He had his work in Kolkata. So he stayed back.

Staying in the West, Sulochana made a steady recovery. She wrote to Navadwip and Kolkata to the effect that she would return home by the end of the month, *Magh*[1], provided her recovery was complete by that time.

It was on the twenty-sixth of *Agrahayana* of the previous year that Hem had gotten married. The same twenty-sixth of *Agrahayana* came back again. Suddenly remembering the date, Guni lifted his face from the book for a few moments and was looking vacantly out the window. Just at that time the newly appointed gatekeeper called out, "Sir, an urgent telegram has come."

Turning his face around Guni found that the gatekeeper had the good sense to bring the postman along. He handed over the envelope, obtained his master's signature and left after saluting him.

Guni was dumbfounded to read the telegram. Hem wrote that she had already set out and she was coming by train from Hoogly. So the carriage must be in the Howrah Railway Station at about three to four in the afternoon. There was no information about why she was coming, who was coming with her, whether Kishori *Babu* was also coming or she was coming alone. There was no woman in the house. Manada had gone to the Western country with Sulochana. So Guni felt a little embarrassed. The coachman, a long-term employee went to the station and came back with Hem before sundown. She had a maid, a servant and a few belongings with her. A shiver ran through

---

1 The tenth month of the Bengali calendar from mid-January to mid-February and the second month of the two-month winter season.

his body when Guni saw Hem. "Pray tell, why have you come dressed like a deranged person?"

Prostrating before him to do *pranam* she said, "Let us go upstairs. I'll tell you then." After sitting down calmly in the upstairs drawing room she asked, "Ma isn't coming back before the end of *Magh.* Isn't it so?"

Guni replied, "That's what she wrote."

"Then there is no point in telling her anything before that. But how strange it is, Guni da. I left for good on this very day a year ago and I also have come back for good on the very same day."

Failing to comprehend the meaning Guni said, "What do you mean by 'Coming back for good?' "

Hem calmly said, "Yes, what else it can be but coming back for good! How could I stay there? Why, can't you understand the situation even from my wearing a plain white sari without any border? All the sacramental rites were finished the day before yesterday and I came back today."

Guni sat there as if a bolt out of the blue had struck him. After a long time he said, "You never gave any indication. What happened to Kishori *Babu*?"

Hem said, "The symptoms of cholera were evident on Wednesday evening. Whatever treatment was possible in that place was given to him. But it was of no avail. The next day, at ten in the morning, he breathed his last."

After a moment or two Guni wiped his tears imperceptibly and said with misty eyes, "Ma will all but die hearing this. It is better not to tell her as long as possible."

Hem said. "Guni da, what can you do? Only I could feel it in my heart that you were conspiring against the will of God. You paid no heed to my entreaty — now wailing and remorse! I am hungry. Can you tell me what can I eat? But I am too tired to cook anything. Let me stave off the hunger for the day with some fruits."

Guni asked, "Didn't you have anything to eat in the morning?"

"No. I had to catch the steamboat in the morning."

Sulochana came back towards the end of *Magh* but without completely recovering from her illness. After coming home and seeing the plight of her daughter she took to the bed on the same day. This grief struck her heart like a thunderbolt. There was no flaw in the treatment and nursing care for her but nothing seemed to have any effect. Then one day Guni became worried to see her hands and feet become bloated. Finding him alone on the same day Sulochana told him, "It is futile to try anymore. Please let me go in peace."

Holding back his tears Guni replied, "It is nothing that serious, Ma, that you should give up all hope."

Sulochana asked, "You tell me what do I have left to hope for?"

Guni sat there with his head bent down.

Sulochana continued, "Guni dear, I am not that dumb. The sin that I consciously committed is, moment by moment, turning my insides into cinders." After remaining silent for a moment or two she added, "Guni, tell me something truly. I know it very well that once you cared for her very much. Couldn't you do the same again if you tried?"

With his head bent down Guni answered, "I always had a soft spot in my heart for her. I cared for her then and I do the same now. You don't have to worry about that. As long as I am alive she will never suffer any hardship."

Sulochana said, "I know it. This is my last blessing to you both and you can tell her about it if need be. Another thing I want to tell you dear. When I was living here Hem wrote me in a letter, *"All the people of Navadwip would be redeemed from sin if they could only have a whiff of the air of the home you are living in now. If you are not earning any merit by living there you won't earn it in heaven itself.* Dear, at this time of my impending death, please bless me so that I may be redeemed of my sin. No one knows the weight of my sin more than I."

Guni began to sob in silence. He really loved Sulochana like his own mother.

Sulochana said, "I won't be able to tell Hem anything. My heart becomes aflame even to look at her face. People tell tales about stepmothers. I am more of an enemy to her than a stepmother could ever be."

The next day she took a turn for the worst. Everyone gave up hope of her survival. At the onset of her labored breathing she called Hem by her side. Touching Hem's chin with her fingers and kissing them she broke into copious sobbing.

"Hem, my love, I am bidding you final farewell!"

Hem, burying her head on her mother's bosom began to cry. After a while Sulochana signaled Hem to sit up. "Don't cry, my dear," she said, "I spent fifteen years in joy and sorrow holding you to my bosom. My time has come today to go to your father. It would be a happy occasion for me had I not devastated your life in this manner I would have gone joyfully and without shedding any tears. I can't even look at your face in my shame and grief, my dear!"

Sobbing, Hem said, "Why are you saying this Ma? Whatever has happened to me was in my destiny. You had no part in it!"

Interrupting her Sulochana responded, "Yes, I had my role in it and I wrote the script myself. You are talking about your bad destiny. There was not a single girl in this country, who had a better destiny than you, if I had not meddled in it and destroyed everything. I know everything and that's why I can't find any consolation anywhere. There are ways of redemption of unperceived sin but where can I find, dear, redemption of a sin committed deliberately?"

Large tear drops of tears began to rain from her eyes. Hem wiped them with the edge of her sari. A little while later Sulochana said, "Don't harbor any resentment against your mother, dear! Lest it becomes inauspicious for you otherwise I would have, at this time of my death, with folded palms, said—"

Hem stopping her at once with her hand and sobbing asked, "Tell me what will make you happy and I will do it. Ma, I have never been disobedient to you."

Sulochana, with utmost effort, placing her numb hand over Hem's head said, "That is what is burning me up, Hem. I told Guni all I wanted to say and he will tell you, if necessary. But change these clothes today. Wear the sari and the jewelry you used to wear a year ago and sit by me on this very bed. Please go and come back wearing the sari and jewelry given by my Guni. Please relieve me of the burden of my sin at least for a while."

Hem got up silently and came back, having obeyed her mother's wish and sat beside her. A hint of a smile seemed to play at the edge of her lips. Sulochana said in a rather composed manner, "The knowledge and understanding that I did not have in thirty-four years of my life I gained in a moment the day I returned from the Western part of the country and saw you for the first time. People talk about the pain of being struck by a thunderbolt. I don't know, dear, how searing that pain is. If half of the pain I felt that day after seeing you is felt from a thunderbolt I don't want it to happen to my worst enemy. Please swear by me, Hem, that you will never stop wearing this kind of clothes and jewelry. I don't know Hem what kind of a stonehearted man ordained our widow's attire. I curse him today that he may have the same searing pain that I suffered. No, no, Hem! Don't stop me today. I won't be able to say anything tomorrow. Let me say it now. May I be happy to see you when I am with your father."

Once more her voice became choked. Hem began to wipe her tears with the edge of her sari. As footsteps were heard approaching from outside, Hem pulled the edge of her sari over her head. Momentarily, Guni, with a *Shahib-* doctor, stood in front of the door. Seeing them, Sulochana said in distress, "Why have you brought another doctor, Guni? After paying his fees send him away and then you come here and sit beside me."

Guni said, "Ma, let him at least feel your—"

"No, Guni! Don't bother me anymore. Let him go."

The *Shahib*-doctor did not understand any of it. Coming into the room he pulled a stool near the bedside and began to get a thermometer out. Annoyed Sulochana said, "Just look at his savvy! He is going to examine my fever with that thing! Be off with him, Guni, and send Nanda to fetch a good *kaviraj*[1]. Let him tell me when

---

[1] An Ayurvedic physician.

it will all be over. Tell her that the physician need not bring any medicine with him."

Sulochana could not stand gaslight, so candles were used in this room. In the evening when the maid lighted the candle-lamp and kept it on the bedside table Sulochana commented, "Tonight must be the last-night. May God punish me more if I can't abandon my sense of shame and guilt and fail to tell the truth, reflecting unity between what is in my heart and what I speak. But let Him not make the innocent suffer! May all suffering resulting from my sin end with my life."

Remaining quiet for a while, suddenly she exclaimed with a sigh "Uh!" as if she was in pain. Hem, lowering her head to her face asked, "Ma, what's the matter?"

Sulochana said slowly, "Nothing in particular, dear. You were not the only one. Even a stone would have melted to see the expression on Guni's face that I had seen. But I didn't and yet what hasn't he done for us! Let bygones be bygones. I won't rehash those anymore. Never disobey him, dear. Never cause any pain to him. Don't you ever forget that God Himself suffers heartache of the likes of him. Whatever is his religion is also yours. This is not my command. It is His command, which made the two of you one forever at the first sight. There is no shame in it, dear! Don't you ever disregard or disobey the One, who knows what are in our hearts and always talks to our hearts. His command sounded in my heart too. But my vanity stopped me from listening to it. I insulted Him by ignoring his command and I am now suffering its consequence. But this is my last entreaty to both of you, dear: don't make my misdeeds last forever by conforming to my wrongful action and my sin."

Manada came in to say that the *kaviraj* has come.

Sulochana said softly, "Let him come in. Hem, would you please go out for while."

## *Five*

Since the death of her mother, amazing changes had occurred in Hem's conduct and behavior. Though she remained close by, physically, yet it felt as if she were withdrawing herself, day by day, further away behind a screen of obscurity. Guni was always a patient and quiet person. He had noticed this change from the very beginning but he was enduring it silently. Only she knew what attracted her to religion. All of a sudden she left novels, poetry and drama books on the shelves and immersed herself completely in the *Ramayana*[1], the *Mahabharata*[1], the *Gita* and the translations of the *Upanishads*[2] into Bengali. Remembering her promise to her mother she was not wearing a simple cotton sari without any border nor did she take off the diamond earrings, the bangles on her wrist and the gold chain round her neck. Otherwise she was rigorously observing all the stern strictures imposed on widows by the society. Abandoning any excess, she ate only once a day, a simple meal cooked by herself. Except for the little time for cooking and doing her minimal household duties Hem began to spend all her time in the pursuit of religion and its practices. If she ever happened to come near Guni and sit beside him she always found some excuse of work and leave shortly. It was apparent from her hasty flights from Guni's sight that she was becoming apprehensive of his company. It was so abundantly clear that Guni would be sitting still and gaze with a vacant look through the window for a long time. As time progressed her observance of even the smallest act of scriptural strictures assumed a major barrier. It was something like the action of a jailer, who creates one barrier after another to keep a high-risk inmate confined to a small space. In the same way Hem was also very

---

[1] One of the two epics of India.

[2] The philosophical portion of the Vedas.

carefully making the movement of a felon in her heart as restricted as possible.

One day she suddenly said, "Guni da shall I take a *mantra?*"

Guni, staring at her face, said, "What kind of a *mantra*? Initiation from a Guru?"

"Yes."

Guni replied with laughter, "You have no reason to fear! And you don't need a new shield everyday for your protection."

Perhaps Hem did not understand the meaning of it. Keeping silent for a moment or two she asked, "Isn't there any need for taking *mantra* from a guru?

Guni answered, "The need is there. But you are not old enough for it. Besides I don't know who is your guru."

Hem responded, "I don't need that kind of a guru. I'll take initiation from you."

Surprised Guni said, "You will take initiation from me! What do I know about initiation, Hem? Moreover you are a Hindu and I am a *Brahmo*."

"I don't know about that," said Hem, "Ma said that whatever is your religion it is mine too. Well Guni da, what does that mean?"

Guni knew what the statement meant. But without coming out with it he said calmly, "Perhaps she meant all religions are same."

Hem replied, "But all religions are not the same."

Keeping silent for a moment or two Guni said, "I don't discuss these matters with outsiders."

Hem responded, "But I am not an outsider."

Guni retorted, "No, you are a special relation of mine. But I won't discuss these matters even with you."

Hem, sighing in disappointment, said, "If you won't tell me how shall I know?"

Observing her face Guni said apologetically, "What do you want to know?"

Hem replied, "The day I ate the leftovers from your plate, ignoring all objections, you told me that I had not done the right thing. One should obey the strictures of one's caste. Today you are telling me all religions are the same. Which one is true?"

"It was a casual statement on that day," said Guni. "Still both statements are true. Caste and religion are not the same thing. One is temporal, dictated by the local or social tradition and the other is eternal, relates to life on earth and hereafter. But following the strictures of religion does not necessarily mean that the rules of caste must also be obeyed. Again it is not true that obeying the rules of caste leads to obeying the strictures of religion. The consequence of not obeying caste rules is suffering. Not everyone can endure it and there is no need for enduring it in all circumstances. That is why I said so the other day." Remaining silent for a few moments he continued, "Hem, these two are different and yet they are entwined. And because they are entwined, with differences in the people of the land there have been differences in religion too. The prime tenet of religion is about life after — death is not the end that is what all say. As a Hindu you are standing on this foundation and I, a *Brahmo,* am also standing on the same foundation. All religions, perhaps, do not believe in the existence of God. But all religions, from the land of the black Africans to Lapland, believe that death does not lead to automatic deliverance. That is why you think of life after death and so do I. It is likely that we think differently but the subject of our thinking is the same. Probably that was Ma's advice to you before her death."

Hem remained silent for a while and then said, "It is not enough to think about it; we must find the path."

Guni said, "Of course, dear, we need to find the path. All problems and conflicts are about finding the path. I do not like your path and you do not like mine. It is a matter of belief and is not subject to proof. That is the reason why there is no end to debates and conflicts. But isn't it the time for you to cook, Hem?"

Hem got up slowly in silence and was on her way. Guni stared at the emptiness with an empty look.

"Guni da!"

Startled, Guni, turning his face asked, "What is it, Hem?"

Hem asked, "Am I following the right path?"

"How can I say, dear? Only you know that. If you are getting happiness and peace then it must be the right path."

"But I am not getting anything."

Guni's eyes were brimming over with tears to hear her pained voice. Somehow controlling himself with difficulty he said softly, "Then why do you do it?"

Hem answered, "I don't know Guni da. Something pulls me, as if by force. It makes me do it and I can not stop."

Guni could not immediately think of an appropriate answer. After a while he said, "Perhaps you are not finding happiness because the path is new to you. You will surely find it in the end."

Hem anxiously asked, "Sure, I'll get it?"

"I am sure. If you can't find peace and happiness in religion where else can you find it? It is my blessing for you that you will be happy in the end."

A couple of days later, in a moonlit night, Guni was lying on the roof on a finely woven mat. Hem came there and sat down near his feet. "Shall I caress your feet, Guni da?"

Guni said, "You may." And then he closed his eyes. He did not dare to look at Hem's face lighted by the moonlight.

While caressing his feet in silence Hem suddenly asked, "Is it appropriate for a widow to marry again, Guni da?

With his eyes closed Guni replied, "What do you say?"

Hem answered, "I didn't come here to say anything, I came to listen."

"Is caressing my feet the prologue for it?"

Hem calmly said, "No, it is not that. When I sit near your feet I can't control the temptation of caressing."

Guni remained silent. He could not trust his tongue.

Hem reminded, "You haven't answered me!"

Guni was still silent.

Hem pinched the sole of his foot and said, "Now answer me quickly."

Guni responded, "I shall. But before I do that you answer me a question"

"What?"

"Did you love your husband?"

"Not a bit. I never even thought of loving him. I didn't bring even a penny's worth of anything from that household and not even one sari given by them. Whatever I ate I gave them four times in return. And this is my relationship with them."

Guni said, "But a chaste woman loves her husband. Should she become a widow, thinking of her husband, she does not re-marry. And at the time of her death, like your mother, she thinks of going to her husband."

Hem responded, "You coerced me into marriage. I am also chaste. So at the time of my death I will also think of going to you. Will I be with you after my death?"

There was no embarrassment, hesitation or even a hint of abashment in her voice; as if some other person was repeating someone else's words. There was nothing in common with the Hem of that earlier time and the Hem of today. Guni was astounded. Hem asked, "Tell me, will I be with you or not?"

Guni answered, "No."

"Why not?"

Guni said, "I don't know where the consequences of my *karma*[1] will take me. You also do not know where the consequences of your *karma* will take you. I may be born as an animal for my bad *karma* and you might be born again as the daughter of a *Brahmin.* Then how will you get me as your husband, dear? If effect of *karma* is pre-determined then the idea of same husband-wife relationship

---

[1] Work, action, deed. Many people mistakenly mean "fate" by this word.

forever can't be true, let alone our imaginary relationship! So much difference, contrast and inequality among people you see all the time. It is perhaps due to *karma.* No force of love can negate it. In this world so many extremely wicked husbands have chaste and devoted wives. According your scripture the husband perhaps will be reborn as a bull. Hem do you wish that his chaste and devoted wife, at the end of her life-long good *karma* to be born as a cow for only to be with husband and live in that cowshed? That can't be. Then there will be no distinction between good and bad deeds. The wife can go to heaven for her own good *karma* and the husband can go to hell for eternity for his bad *karma.* No amount of wishing can bring them together."

Remaining silent for a long time Hem said, "Then truly is there no way to be together?"

Guni said, "No. There is no need for it either. The union that is the best of all, if you can be with that One when you will not even have the desire to be with anyone else and at the same time it fulfils all other desires for union is far better, Hem. You strive for that union, Hem. I sincerely bless you that no one takes you away from that path. May all the pains which we have inflicted on you, be someday washed out completely!"

Hem could see in the moonlight that teardrops were rolling down Guni's cheeks. With her head bowed down she touched his feet to do *pranam.* She got up and slowly went away. In this manner she had left in silence many times before. But today she left after shattering the wall of Guni's self-restraint to its foundation. He began to stew in self-pity thinking that the good fortune he had coveted all his life had just floated away before his very eyes and that he hadn't even stretched out his hand to grab it. He didn't have even a shred of doubt in the depth of Hem's love for him. Today he had heard it loud and clear from her own lips and yet he could not voice his own feelings. Since Sulochana's death he had thought of expressing it many times but never uttered it. All the time he thought to his heart that a venomous serpent was asleep and it would stand up, flaring its hood, with the touch of his hand. The fear that had held him back many times before did not let him stretch his hands that day either.

After taking a bath in the morning Hem used to come to do *pranam* everyday. As soon as she came in next morning Guni, overcoming all his hesitation with extreme effort asked, "Hem, why did you ask about remarriage of widows yesterday?"

Hem answered, "I read about it in the newspaper and that was the reason."

Guni asked again, "Do you think of it as good?"

Hem replied in a few words, "The shame of it! How can you call it a real marriage?"

Guni asked, "Why not? All religions in this world but Hinduism permit remarriage of widows."

"Let them have it." So saying, Hem was about to leave when Guni called out after her to say, "I have something else to ask you, Hem."

Hem, turning back, asked, "What?"

"How old are you?"

"Sixteen."

"Will you live like a female ascetic all your life from this age?"

With a faint smile on her face Hem replied, "What else can I do? It is in my destiny. And as ordained by your wisdom!"

Guni stared at her face for a moment and said, "Isn't there any other path? Isn't there any other solution?"

"Nothing at all, Guni da. Nothing at all!" Saying which Hem left the room.

As time marched on, every iota of Hem's body was brimming with youthfulness. And her devotion to religious practices began to surpass her youthfulness. Guni noticed everything but could not marshal enough courage to ask any question. There was something in Hem that intimidated everyone. Even her mother had been scared of her and Guni was as well. A few days after the above exchange Guni was getting ready for the court one day when Hem came into the room. Unlocking the chest of drawers she got the bank checkbook out and handing it over to Guni she said, "On your way back, please bring five-hundred rupees with you."

"Very well," Guni said and kept the checkbook in his pocket.

Hem said, "Wait a minute. The money for household expenses is about to run out. Bring an extra two-hundred with it."

Surprised, Guni asked, "Then what are the five-hundred rupees for?"

Hem answered, "Oh, that money! I am going to Varanasi tomorrow."

Guni sat down on the stool and said, "You are going to Varanasi tomorrow! Didn't you even think of discussing the matter with anyone?"

Embarrassed, Hem replied, "I intended to get your permission first."

Guni said, "You have already made the decision, so when do you think that you would get permission? Who else is going with you?"

Hem responded, "Manada, Nanda, and the gatekeeper are going with me. I was going to ask for your permission tonight. Guni da, will you come with us tomorrow?"

"Very well, I'll go." So saying Guni left for the court house.

In the evening Hem, after keeping the money in the locked cupboard drawer, came to Guni and said, "We can't go tomorrow."

"Why?"

"A telegram came from the Brahmin cook's home today at noon hour. His mother is seriously ill. I have paid him three months' salary and gave him leave of absence. He has already left for his home."

"Who is going to cook?"

"I'll do the cooking until we can find a cook. Guni da, do get married!"

"Why?"

"There is no "why" about it. If you'll not marry who will run the household? And who is going to look after you?"

"You."

Laughing, Hem asked, "Do you think that I'll bear the burden of this household forever? Don't I have to do any work?"

"Isn't looking after me work?"

Hem said with smile, "I can't win a debate with you. No, that won't do at all. Grown up women are available in your society. Chose one and get married to her. Giving her the charge of the house I'll go to Varanasi."

Guni said, "You marry someone and I'll do the same."

Hem was smiling so long. All her smile evaporated in a trice. She said somberly, "What a shame! What kind of a joke is that? I don't want to hear such a thing from you again!"

Guni could not say anything anymore. He became silent, staring at her face. Hem left the

room.

## *Six*

Hem stayed in Varanasi for about two months. When she learned of Guni's illness Hem returned home. Had she not come back the illness could have become serious. But she nursed him to almost full recovery within a short period of time.

It was raining in torrents outside. Sitting up on his bed Guni was watching the downpour through the windowpanes. And he was thinking about Hem. One particular change in her caught his attention. Previously Hem used to do *pranam* everyday but she was no longer coming to do that. He had sent Manada for calling Hem. Coming back, Manada reported that she was busy with telling her beads along with God's name.

About two hours later, entering the room Hem asked, "Were you calling me?"

Guni answered, "Yes, please sit down for a moment."

Hem responded, "But I haven't yet finished telling my beads along with God's name."

"Wasn't two hours enough for it?"

"What can you do in mere two hours? My guru has directed me to repeat God's name at least two thousand times."

"Guru directed? Who is this guru?"

Hem responded, "This time I have taken *mantra* in Varanasi. My guru is an ascetic, living in Varanasi. Seeing him, one does not have any desire to return to family life. I only think of how soon I would again see his lotus feet. I am contemplating on going back tomorrow or the day after."

After remaining silent for a while Guni said, "How can you go back tomorrow or the day after? I have not recovered completely yet, Hem. Who is going to look after me?"

Slightly embarrassed, Hem responded, "That's nothing. It will take only a day or two."

Guni pleaded, "You will have to stay at least those two days."

"Very well, I'll stay." Saying which Hem was about to leave when Guni called after her and added, "On second thought, you may go tomorrow or the day after but when will you be returning?"

"I don't think that I'll be returning soon. You can send me one hundred rupees per month and that will be enough but anything less won't do."

Guni responded, "I am not talking about money, Hem. Instead of one hundred I'll send you two hundred, if needed. But are you not coming back indeed?"

"What for shall I come back?"

"Would you come back if you heard of my death?"

Aggrieved, Hem responded, "What kind of a question is that, Guni da?"

Guni continued, "Nothing can be taken for granted, dear. That's why I am telling you in advance. I shall make provision of money for you in my will. And this house will also be yours. If you ever come back, stay in this house and sleep in this room. This is my request to you."

Hem was about to say something. Instead she opined, "I am telling you Guni da, you have nothing to worry about. You are still weak and that's why you are having these thoughts."

"Perhaps that's it." Saying which he resumed watching the rain outside. Hem left the room with a disheartened look on her face.

A little after evening, looking into the room from outside the door and finding it dark, enraged Hem called out, "Nanda, didn't you light the lamp in Babu's room?"

Guni responded from inside the room, "I told her not to."

Running, Nanda appeared there. Sending her out to get a lighted gaslight and visualizing in the dark where Guni's feet might be, Hem sat there on the bed. After Nanda left, leaving a light in the room, as Hem touched Guni's feet he moved them away from her at once. Aggrieved, Hem pleaded, "Won't you let me touch your feet anymore?"

Guni answered, "There is no need for that. Probably it has been forbidden by your guru."

Hem understood that Guni had noticed that she had never touched his feet since she came back. But she could say nothing in response either and remained silent. After a while she asked, "Guni da, are you angry with me?"

"Have I ever been angry with you, Hem?"

Regretting at once, Hem responded, "No. never — but why did you talk about those things today?"

"Which things, dear?"

"About your will and a lot more. I am telling you Guni da, you will recover completely and you have nothing to fear."

Guni commented with a gentle smile, "Do you think that I am afraid of not getting well?"

On the verge of sobbing, Hem answered, "I beseech you please do not talk like that. How shall I survive if you don't recover completely."

"How can I live if you go away for good? Suppose I hold you back and don't let you go!"

Remaining silent for a few moments Hem responded, "What would you gain by holding me back?"

"Gain!" Guni could not say anymore. He remained silent. The large raindrops were beating against the windowpanes, making a loud "tap, tap, tap" sound. At times, gusts of high wind coming into the room were almost snuffing out the gaslight. The dim chatter of the servants was coming from the ground floor. Yet the two sat there in silence. Since childhood Guni had much self-restraint but he easily felt hurt, ashamed and embarrassed. He had built his dam of patience very strongly. But Sulochana's last blessing, from that very day, was gnawing a hole in its foundation like a mouse and letting the flood water in and causing damage to a wide area of the dam to such an extent that the whole dam could crumble any time. While watching the fury of Nature outside he wanted to think out the entire conversation of that day. But his ill health and weak mind did not allow him to clearly understand anything.

Suddenly Hem said, "Guni da, why are you silent? What are you thinking?"

"Nothing! Nothing at all! I can't tell you what is on my mind. You won't understand it. But if you ever change your opinion and I am alive — do come back."

Moving away a little, Hem responded, "I understand it all. What a twist of fate! The protector has now turned into a predator! In the end it is you who want to drag me into perdition!"

Guni had been leaning back against an oversize pillow. There was fire in his eyes. Sitting straight up he boomed, "Shame on you, Hem! Think before you speak. What are you saying?"

Standing up with lightning speed Hem retorted, "I thought it out all right before speaking. What you are saying in a round about way I am saying to your face. You want to degrade me! How can a widow be married again, Guni da? I am not such a child that pretending to follow the path of religion I'll slide into the path of sin. I do not want your money, I do not want your protection, and I want absolutely nothing from you. I would rather return to my father-in-law's home and do menial work for food and shelter. But I have no use for this opulence. Heaven forbid that I ever have such inclination! Where did you leave your intelligence on that day? Why couldn't you say it as clearly as you did today?"

Sitting calmly, Guni answered, "Hem, I've committed an offence. Please forgive me. I am sick — think of it."

"I have thought indeed. If I can't forgive you today I'll do so tomorrow. But I won't keep any connection with you. Tomorrow I'll return to the place, which I left one day out of vain pride. I'll hang on to that place at all costs and think of it as my Varanasi, my heaven itself. You also forgive me Guni da. I am on my way now."

Hem left. Straightening himself, Guni sat there — just like a fanpalm tree that has just been struck by a thunderbolt — lifeless and burnt out from inside but standing right up. He had no energy left in him to even slump to the bed.

## *Seven*

Once more, it was the time for Durga Puja. Opening the window in the early morning, and standing still, Hem was gazing at the red glow of the rising sun in the east. A serenade of *sanai*[1] and other accompaniments playing the doleful tune, bibhash and melting into all of autumn's tenderness were slowly flooding Hem's entire being. Unbeknown to her, tears were raining from her eyes. She had not heard any news about Guni for a long time — she thought to herself, 'Who knows where her Guni da was now and how he was doing!' At the time of her departure, sobbing, Guni had pleaded, "Hem, stay back for a day or two. Don't leave in an angry mood." The tears of the one who felt hurt, ashamed and embarrassed had no value to her on that day. Guni had come down all the way to the roadside with his suffering and sick body and entreated, "Hem, your mind can not be in its normal state. For some reason it is utterly distressed. So I beseech you to come back and stay at least for a day." Without paying any heed and getting into the carriage Hem sat there. Coming close to the window of the carriage Guni had pleaded for the last time, "Hem, this act of yours will perhaps always strike you like a thunderbolt. I am not saying this for my sake, dear, I am saying it for your welfare. Please come down from the carriage only for today." Hem had responded by ordering the coachman to drive on.

Coming back to the bed and sobbing copiously she had made her hair all wet with pouring tears and then she fell asleep. There was a reason for so much grief. The day before she had sent the maid to the manager to give her only fifty rupees to go for a pilgrimage. The manager sent her back empty-handed but with the message that he could not give her any money without the permission of *Chotobabu.*

---

1 A wind instrument like an oboe, often played at weddings and other ceremonies.

Hem did not speak face to face with her brother-in-law. But she had told from behind the door, "Can't the manager give me fifty rupees if I ask?"

The brother-in-law had answered, "No. You are entitled to have only room and board but no cash."

Hem had responded, "I know very well, *thakurpo*[1], what I am entitled to or not! I did not come here to squabble with you over money nor have I the inclination to take legal action. But don't you take me to be absolutely helpless. If you wish to you can give. If not, I can assure that if money has any power, as an adversary I'll take the bricks of your house, one by one, and throw them into the Ganges over there."

In a little while the money had come but Hem did not accept it. In sheer outrage she had thrown the money all over the courtyard and then, locking her room, she sprawled on her bed. All day she did not eat, nor did she get up. Remembering someone, she began to cry.

It was past seven when she woke up. Taking her bath she had just sat down to say her prayers to God when the maid brought the news, "Bouma[2], four or five people from your brother's home have come bearing gifts for you." As she was saying this Manada came in and did *pranam.* Taking just one look at her face and forgetting it all she twined her hands round her neck and began to cry like a child. Ever since the previous day her eyes had not been dry. All of a sudden when she found Manada the tears that she had been holding back for nearly one year came out like a flood and washed it all away.

Taking Manada into her room she asked, "Give me the letter Guni da has sent."

Manada responded, "He didn't send any."

Disbelieving, she questioned, "Didn't send?"

"No, *didimani*[3]. Can he sit up to write letters?"

---

[1] A younger brother of one's husband, a brother-in-law.

[2] A son's wife, a daughter-in-law; a younger brother's wife, a sister-in-law.

[3] A lady.

Ashen, Hem asked, "He can't sit up! What has happened to him?"

"Haven't you heard anything?"

"No, tell me."

Manada began, "What is there to say?" And she began to sob.

Irritated Hem retorted, "You can cry later. Now tell me what has happened."

Sobbing, she added, "There is nothing much to say, didi[1]. The day after you left he came down with fever. He gets well and then comes down with fever. This has been repeated many times — I don't think that we'll see him alive when we get back."

Hem urged, "Go on!"

Manada continued, "Then from Baddhaman or some such place a *mashi*[2] appeared. Then her husband, son and his wife, daughter and her husband and now no one is left behind. There is no room unoccupied in the house."

"I will throw all of them out — then what?"

"They are eating well and having a good time. And Babu is lying in his bed upstairs, without any doctor or any other kind of physician. Neither medicine nor any nourishment! It seems a change of air will do him good but who is going to take him?"

Hem responded, "What are all of you doing? Why did not Nanda take him?"

Striking her forehead with her palm, distressed Manada answered, "He was the servant who served Babu for the longest period. *Mashi's* son, Abhay, beat him up and threw him out. He drinks a lot. There are times when he makes so much trouble in his drunken condition that no one dares to face him. Even Babu is afraid of him."

---

[1] Elder sister, elder female cousins, and other elder women of the same generation and between grandparents and granddaughters.

[2] A sister or a cousin sister of one's mother, an aunt.

Remaining silent for a moment or two Hem asked, "Manu, tell me the truth, didi, will not my Guni da live any longer?"

Manada replied, "Why shouldn't he live? With good treatment and care he will get well for sure — but how long can he survive if he is left in that condition?"

Hem sat there for about a minute with her eyes closed and then standing up she asked, "Manada, do you have enough money with you for going back?"

"Indeed we have it, didi! You know that Babu always sends with ten rupees when only one is needed — I have it right here with me." She showed the notes tied in a knot in a corner of her sari's edge.

Hem asked, "When will you leave? Tomorrow?"

Manada answered, "Yes didi, we'll have to leave tomorrow. I am the only one left from the old days, the rest are all new. No one can stay long. The *mashi*, her husband, her son, daughter, daughter-in-law — all are same, as if the Creator made all of them in the same mold on a special order. They say that I am a hard nut to crack and that is why I am still hanging by a thread. That guy, Abhay, even came tried to thrash me. About Babu he says — the sooner he dies the better it is!"

Hem's eyes were aflame. "First let me go there. Do you know when the steamer is returning?"

"In about an hour," Manada answered, "I got the information from the quay."

"Then we'll go by that one. Go and fetch a carriage."

"Will you go, didi? But today is not an auspicious day."

"It is a good day. Don't waste time and just fetch a carriage."

That same afternoon the mother was serving food to her son, Abhay, and cajoling him to eat two more *luchis*[1]. The staircase to the third floor was just beside them. Seeing the stranger, Hem, the surprised *mashi* asked, "Who are you, dear?"

---

[1] Round flat bread made from bleached wheat flour and deep fried.

Answering, "I am from a different land," Hem went up. Abhay was gawking at her exquisite beauty like a wolf.

Entering Guni's room Hem found him lying down, facing the wall. She could not figure out whether he was awake or sleeping. The bunch of keys was lying beside his head. First of all she knotted it in a corner of the edge of her sari. Reading the labels on a couple of open medicine bottles on a table she found that the date had passed fifteen days ago. She understood the whole situation very clearly. Then opening the iron chest, she was beginning to compare the signature on the used checks with that of Guni's, when the *mashi*, entering the room, was dumbfounded. She barked, "Who are you to open the iron chest?"

Hem answered, "Why are you shouting? You'll wake him up."

*Mashi*, cranking her voice a few notches higher asked, "Why am I shouting?"

Guni was awake and he turned around. Hem answered, "If I won't open it who shall? You?"

None of the two noticed that Guni was watching all this. *Mashi* was getting very much agitated.

Guni asked softly, "Hem, when did you come, dear?"

"Just now. Please make it clear to her that no outsider should yell when I open your things. Make her understand that all these things are *mine*. Please ask her to leave."

Guni got the picture. Laughing, he said, "Because of that claim have you come after so long to open the chest?"

While counting the pages of the checks Hem grunted, "Uh-huh!"

*Mashi* asked, "Who is she, Guni?"

"My sister." On hearing the answer, a shock wave ran through Hem's spine. Lifting her head up for a moment she sat there gazing at the floor.

*Mashi* said, "Never heard any such talk until now. What kind of a sister is she?"

Avoiding any direct answer Guni curtly stated, "She left after a tiff with me — but everything belongs to her."

*Mashi* did not believe it nor did she understand it — slowly she left. After she left and without taking a good look at Hem's face Guni said, "Why did you have this sudden whim just before my death?" Saying this and after observing her face Guni became very much contrite. The last trace of blood was drained out of Hem's face — as if, suddenly she has been turned into a stone statue by the curse of an outraged ascetic. With trepidation Guni called, "Hem!"

Hem did not respond, nor even moved — she just sat there, staring at the floor with unblinking eyes.

Extremely worried, Guni called out again, "Hem, listen to me."

In response, Hem released a deep sigh and remained unmoved. Guni somehow sat up on the bed and got down from it. With utmost strain, slowly coming in front of Hem, he stood there. Prostrating at once and burying her face between his feet Hem cried out, "Everybody punishes me for no good reason. I never thought in my wildest dream that you, too, would do the same."

Guni was speechless. He remained motionless for a few moments with his eyes transfixed at Hem's ink black disheveled hair, covering his feet like the dark clouds covering the *Sravana* sky. Then sitting down slowly and keeping his right hand on Hem's head he calmly said, "How could I punish you Hem. I didn't even punish myself for your loving me. This is not punishment, dear sister. On the last day of my impending end I'll give you the priceless gift of peace that I got after four years of untold grief and suffering. Let us go to Varanasi."

Keeping her head buried and still crying Hem responded, "Let us go. But is this your last directive! Will I be able to bear it?"

Guni answered, "You surely will. You will be able to bear it when you will realize that to glorify Love, estrangement has always come to the doors of the likes of you, endowed with opulent adoration and divine grace instead of begging at the cottage of the miserly lover. When you will know that unsatiated yearning is the heart of great love. With this it has gained immortality and through the ages stored for us untold poetry and priceless honeyed tears. You will be able to bear when you'll realize without any doubt why a *Viashnava's* heart is the hundred years' of pain of Radha's estrangement from her lover. Come now and sit up. Let us go to Varanasi on this very day. The few days that I have left are for receiving your last service. With God's blessings it will remain undiminished forever and point you to the right path and keep you in peace."

# Bindu's Son

(*Bindur Chhele*)

In *Bindu's Son* (Bindur Chhele) the love of an aunt, Bindu, is depicted as stronger than that between the birthmother, Annapurna, and her child, Amulya. The conflict and tension in the plot is anchored to Bindu's love and affection for *her* son and her extreme concern for his welfare. The strength of the story lies in utter simplicity in style and setting and in the control of every detail of the carefully crafted life-like characters. The story paints poverty with pathological accuracy and life with all its complexity in a joint family in early twentieth century Bengal.

## *One*

Jadab Mukhujje and Madhab Mukhujje had forgotten that they were not born of the same mother, and so had outsiders. Impoverished Jadab, suffering much hardship, saw to it that his brother passed his law exam and after much striving he succeeded to bring Bindubasini, the only daughter of a wealthy landowner, as his sister-in-law. Bindubasini was exceptionally beautiful. Tears of joy rolled down the cheeks of *barobou*[1], Annapurna, the first day she came into the household with this incomparable beauty and ten thousand rupees worth of paper notes. As there was no mother-in-law or any other sister-in-law she was the lady of the house. Holding up the face of the *chhotobou* Annapurna declared to the neighbors that such was the only kind of bride worthy of bringing into a home. She had the likeness of Lakshmi[2], the goddess of good fortune. But the error in her judgment caught up with her in a few days. By that time she became aware that the *chhotobou* had brought with her four times as much vanity and feeling of hurt, shame and embarrassment as beauty and money.

One day Annapurna told her husband in confidence, "My dear, beguiled by her beauty and the bag of money the *bou*[3] that you brought home is nothing but a venomous serpent!"

Jadab did not believe a word of it. Scratching his head and muttering, "Is that so!" a couple of times, he left for his work.

Jadab had a very calm disposition. He worked as an administrator in the estate of a landlord and after coming home he was busy with his religious practices and rituals. Madhab was younger than his elder brother by ten or twelve years. After becoming a lawyer he had just begun his practice.

---

[1] The eldest brother's wife.

[2] The goddess of wealth.

[3] A married woman.

Approaching her he confided, "*Bouthan*[1], when did money become so important to *dada*[2]? Had he waited for a while could I not have earned it?" Annapurna remained silent.

There was another risky matter at hand. There was no way to manage *chhotobou*. She used to have such severe bouts of fainting that they would scare the wits out of everyone in the house and there was no other way but to call in a doctor. So everyone was convinced that the much-coveted matrimonial alliance was a great blunder. Only Jadab refused to give up. Standing up to everyone else he frequently asserted, "No, it can't be. Wait and you will see. My Ma is as beautiful as the Supreme Mother. Can all this be for nothing? This can never be so."

One day Annapurna was frightened out of her wits to see *chhotobou*, after exchange of a few words, sitting still with a glum face. Suddenly thinking of something and picking her one and a half year old son, Amulyacharan, who was fast asleep she threw him on Bindu's lap and quickly ran away from there.

Amulya, awakened from his sleep, began to cry.

Bindu, trying her utmost to get hold of herself, came out of her swoon and holding the little boy to her bosom went into her room.

Annapurna saw it all, hiding from her view, and became delighted to discover an unfailing miracle-cure for fainting spell.

Since the whole burden of running the household rested on Annapurna's shoulders she could not give adequate attention to raising her son. Moreover, she would feel unwell if she could not get a good night's sleep after a day's hard work. So *chhotobou* assumed this responsibility for the little boy.

One morning, about a month later, carrying Amulya in her arms and entering the kitchen she asked, "*Didi*[1], where is the milk for my Amulyadhan?"

---

[1] Elder brother's wife.

[2] Elder brother or cousin. It is extended to other elder men out of affection or courtesy. It is also an affectionate term for addressing grandfather or a grandfather-like figure.

Annapurna left aside the work at hand and responded with trepidation, "Just wait a minute, dear. I'll have it boiled in no time."

Bindu was already incensed as she entered the kitchen.

She spoke in an acrid tone, "I told you even yesterday that I must have the milk by eight o'clock. Now it is nine. You can spell it out to me if it is too much for you. I can make some other arrangement. And you, the daughter of a good Brahmin, can't you be a bit more mindful. Maybe the grub for all other people in the house would have been delayed by a minute or two."

*Bamunthakrun,* the lady Brahmin-cook, remained silent.

Annapurna suggested, "We could be mindful too if the only work we had was to apply cosmetics, such as mascara and dot on the forehead of a son. Can't you wait for a minute, *chhotobou*?"

*Chhotobou* answered, "In God's name, *didi*, I beseech you never to touch Amulya's milk and I also vow not to ask you again."

So saying she dropped Amulya on the floor and picking up a wok placed it on the cooking fire. At this unexpected turn of events Amulya let out a loud cry. Bindu, pinching his cheek asserted, "Shut up you scoundrel, I'll beat the living daylights out of you if you yell again." The maid of the house, came running and as she was going to pick up the boy Bindu thundered, "Go away! Be off with you from my sight!"

She could not advance any further. She stood there, frozen.

Bindu didn't say a word to anyone. She picked up her crying son and began to boil the milk.

Annapurna stood there motionless. A little later, after Bindu left with the milk she said, addressing the cook, "Did you listen to her talk? The other day I jokingly told her that she could have Amulya. Taking that literally, *chhotobou* today forbade me in God's name!"

From then on, Bindubasini began to raise Annapurna's son. The consequence was that Amulya began to address his aunt as "Ma" and his mother as "didi".

---

[1] Elder sister, elder female cousins, and other elder women of the same generation and between grandparents and granddaughters.

## *Two*

One morning, about four years later, the day after Amulya's sacrament of initiation into his student life, when Annapurna was busy in the kitchen Bindubasini called after her from outside, "*Didi*, Amulya has come to do *pranam*[1] to you. Please come out for a minute."

Annapurna was amazed to see the way Amulya was dressed up. He had mascara on his eyes, a dot between his brows, a gold chain adorning his neck and his hair tied in a ponytail on his head. He was wearing a piece of cloth, dyed yellow. A clay inkpot tied with twine thread was hanging from his one hand and a few palmyra leaves rolled in a small mat were under his other arm.

Bindu said, "Do *pranam* to didi, my darling!"

Amulya did *pranam* to his mother.

He was wearing no shoes, socks or any foreign-style clothes. Looking at this strange attire Annapurna laughed and commented, "Such fancies come to your head, *Chhotobou*! Your son is going to school, I suppose."

Bindu responded with a smile, "Yes, I am sending him to the primary school of Ganga Pundit. Bless him, *didi*, may this day be fruitful in his life."

Turning to the servant she instructed, "Bhairab, on my behalf tell Pundit Mashay to ensure that no one beats my son."

"Didi, take these five rupees. Arrange a nice big platter of uncooked food together with this money and send Kadam with this gift to the school." Saying which she kissed her son with deep affection and left with him in her arms.

---

1 An act of veneration (by a Hindu) in which a younger person touches the feet of an elder in order to be blessed by the propitious dust. Also, sometimes the simple act of folding one's palms before another person or a deity.

The two eyes of Annapurna were brimming over with tears. Addressing the *bamunthakrun* she remarked, "She is always busy with the son. God only knows what she would have done if she were the birth-mother!"

The cook said, "May be that's why God didn't give her one. She is now eighteen or nineteen—"

She could not finish the sentence. Coming back alone *Chhotobou* said, "Didi, can't you talk *batthakur*[1] into opening a school in front of our house? I'll pay all expenses."

Annapurna couldn't help laughing. She added, "He hasn't even taken two steps away from you, *chhotobou,* and by this time you have changed your mind! Why don't you also go and sit in the school!"

Embarrassed, Bindu said with a smile, "It is not that I have changed my mind, didi. I am thinking of the difference between keeping him out of sight and keeping an eye on him. The other students are naughty. Finding him a wee little boy they might thrash him."

Annapurna responded, "It may be so. Children get into fights all the time. Besides all children are equally precious, *chhotobou.* If the other parents can bear to send their children to school why can't you?"

Bindu didn't like comparison with others at all. Perhaps becoming unhappy in her mind she answered, "You always say the same thing, didi. Suppose someone jabs his pen into his eyes — then what would happen?"

Reading the state of her mind and laughing, Annapurna responded, "Then you'll take him to a doctor. But I am telling you the truth that I could never have thought about someone jabbing him in the eye even if I raked my brains for seven days and seven nights in a row. So many children go to school but I never heard of anyone being jabbed in the eye."

Bindu responded, "Just because you haven't heard of it, does it mean that it can never happen? Who can foretell an accident? Very well, why don't you broach the subject with him and then we'll see what happens?"

---

[1] Husband's eldest brother.

Annapurna solemnly answered, "I can see already what is going to happen. When the idea has caught your fancy you won't let it go without actually doing it! I'll not be able to talk about such unheard-of matters. It is not that you don't talk to him so why don't you propose it yourself?"

Piqued, Bindu answered this time, "Certainly I'll propose it. I can't send my son so far away everyday— whether someone likes it or not and whether he gets an education or not! And you, Kadam, didn't I ask you to take the platter of uncooked food? Why are you still standing there, gawking?"

Observing her angry demeanor anxious Annapurna responded, "I'm making the platter ready right away. Don't be so worried, *chhotobou*! Don't you think that he is going to grow up? Would you be able to keep him dependent on you all the time? Why don't you think of that?"

Without answering *chhotobou* instructed, "Kadam, after offering him the platter of food and giving a few grains of dust from his feet on the boy's head bring him back. And invite Pundit Mashay to come here this afternoon. How can I make someone understand who is unwilling to do so? I am telling her that someone may hurt him because he a little child. And she is telling me if I would be able to keep him dependent on me forever! I didn't come here to seek advice on whether I would be able to do that or not." Saying which, she left in a huff.

Astounded Annapurna just stood there.

Kadam opined, "Ma, don't stand there any longer. Perhaps, she may come back right away. Once she has made up her mind not even God can stop her."

That evening, *barokarta*[1], after taking his opium and lying on the bed on his side he was gently puffing on his *hookah* to speed up his level of intoxication. Just at that moment the iron chain on the door jangled.

Opening his eyes with some effort Jadab responded, "Who is there?"

---

[1] The eldest brother or the head of the (joint) family.

Entering the room Annapurna announced, "*Chhotobou* has come to tell you something, listen carefully."

Jadab sitting up in a hurry asked, *Chhoto* Ma[1]? What is it, Ma?'

He loved *Chotobou*[2] dearly. But *chhotobou* did not talk. Annapurna said on her behalf, "Other children might jab her son's eye. So she wants you to set up a primary school right in our house."

Throwing the pipe in his hand away, horrified, Jadab asked, "Who jabbed him? Let me see what, how did it happen?"

Giving back the pipe in his hand Annapurna said laughingly, "No one has done it yet. Just in case it happens."

Calming down Jadab responded, "Oh, you are talking hypothetically! I thought it —"

Standing unobserved, enraged Bindu said softly, "*Didi*, didn't you say that you couldn't broach any unheard-of matter? Then why are you talking about it now?"

Annapurna herself understood that the manner of her raising the matter was not appropriate and that its consequence wouldn't be pleasant. The deeper implication of this soft tone became quite clear to her and she really became frightened. All her indignation fell on her innocent husband and she aimed her sharp comments at him. "People shut their eyes from opium intoxication. Do they shut their ears too?" she told. "Just look at what I said and what he heard! 'Let me see what?' and 'how did it happen!' Did I say that someone has made Amulya blind? I am beleaguered from all sides!"

Uninvolved Jadab's tipsy state from his opium intake was about to evaporate. Bewildered, he asked, "Why? What happened?"

Piqued Annapurna answered, 'Whatever has happened?' Splendid indeed! It is nothing but a hassle to discuss something with the likes of you. It must be the effect of some misdeed I had done in the past." Saying which, she angrily left the scene.

Jadab said, "You tell me, Ma, clearly what has happened."

Bindu, standing behind the door said softly, "If there was a primary school by the granary outside..."

---

[1] The youngest mother figure (aunt).

[2] The youngest brother's wife.

Jadab interjected, "That is not a big thing! But where will you find students for it?"

Bindu answered, "Pundit Mashay came this afternoon. He said that he would bring his primary school here for ten rupees a month. I suggest that this expense be paid from my accumulated interest income."

Pleased, Jadab responded, "Very good, Ma. I'll engage someone tomorrow to expedite it. It would be a good idea if Gangaram would transfer his primary school here."

Bindu's anger melted away at her elder brother-in-law's consent. Entering the kitchen with a smiling face she found Annapurna sitting there with a glum face and Kadam, sitting by her side, explaining something animatedly. As Bindu entered, her face turned wan and washed out. She said, "It is you I see!" And abruptly ended there. Bindu understood that they were talking about her. Coming closer she asked, "Tell me, what are you saying about me?"

Her throat was bone dry in fear. Swallowing a gulp she answered, "No didi, nothing much, *baro* Ma was saying, supposing…."

Bindu said curtly, "I can suppose. You go and mind your own business."

Without saying another word Kadam left with great relief.

Then Bindu said to Annapurna, "*Baroginni's*[1] advisors are great indeed. Someone should get their salaries increased by petitioning to *batthakur*."

Bindu used to address Annapurna as *baroginni* when she was displeased and as *didi* when she was pleased.

Aflamed Annapurna retorted, "Why don't you go and petition? As if *batthakur* will chop off my head! And you got a *batthakur*, who is just made to measure! He would at once begin — what is it Ma! What is on your mind Ma! You said it right, Ma! — I have seen many lucky people but none like you, *chhotobou*. Under what a lucky star you were born, my god, every one in the house is scared stiff of you!"

---

[1] Eldest brother's wife in a joint family of more than one brother.

Bindu was displeased indeed but she burst out laughing at the way Annapurna was talking. She added, "But you aren't scared of me!"

Annapurna responded, "Aren't I ever! There has not yet been born a human whose blood wouldn't run cold to see your face in your furious mood! But *chhotobou,* it is not nice for you to be so hot-tempered! You are no longer a little girl! If you were bearing children you could have been, by now, the mother of four or five boys. How can I blame you? That old man has spoiled you rotten by smothering you with his affection."

Bindu affirmed, "I agree with you, *didi,* that I was born under a lucky star. Many people get wealth, love and affection. These are not uncommon. But one must accumulate, over many lives, merits by ascetic practices to get a god-like elder brother-in-law. This was in my destiny and what can you do about it with your jealousy? But he did not spoil me with his affection. If anyone has spoiled me it is none but you."

Waving her hands in denial Annapurna asserted, "Me? No one can say anything like that about me. I am a strict disciplinarian — but what can I do? It is my bad luck that no one is intimidated by me. Even the maids and servants argue with me, right to my face, on equal terms, as if they are the masters and mistresses and I am their maid! Because of what I am I tolerate it. If it were any one else —"

Bindu burst into laughter at her inconsistent statement and added, "Didi, you are a person from another era when righteousness ruled supreme. I don't know why you were born in this era. Why? No one dares to argue with me!" Saying which kneeling in front of her and twining her arms round her neck she entreated her, "*Didi,* tell me a story!"

Irritated Annapurna commanded, "Go, go away from here!"

Kadam came running to inform, "*Didi,* your Amulyadhan, cut his hand in the nut-cracker and is crying now."

Bindu, at once letting go of her arms, and standing up asked, "Where did he get the nut-cracker? And what were you doing?"

"I was making the bed in the other room, didi. I don't even know when he went into *baro* Ma's room and —"

"Well done! He has done well indeed! Be off with you." Saying which, Bindu left the room. In a little while she returned, carrying Amulya, with a wet bandage wrapped around a finger, in her arms and she said, "*Didi*, I have told you many times to keep nut-crackers and all carefully put away when there is a child, in particular, in the house. But—"

Getting even more irritated Annapurna responded, "What you are saying *chhotobou,* make no sense whatsoever. Just because your son may sometime go into the room and cut his finger, shall I keep the nut-cracker locked up in an iron chest?"

Bindu answered, "No! From tomorrow I'll keep him tied with a rope so that he can't enter your room." Saying which, she went out.

Annapurna commented, "Did you hear it, Kadam, how overbearing is her pronouncement! Do people keep nut-crackers in iron chest?"

Kadam was going to say something but she stopped with her mouth wide open.

Coming back Bindu asserted, "I am warning you. If you'll ever again use the likes of maids as arbiters I'll, for sure, leave this place and go to my parents' home with my son."

Annapurna shot back, "Go right away. But keep it in mind that I'll never even talk about bringing you back."

"I won't even want to come back." So saying, Bindu left with a gloomy face.

A couple of hours later Annapurna entered *chhotobou's* room with heavy steps. In one corner of the room Madhab Chandra was reading his case files on a small table, and, lying down on the bed nearby, Bindu was telling stories in a soft voice to Amulya. Annapurna announced, "Come and eat your dinner."

Bindu responded, "I am not hungry."

Amulya, twining his arms round her aunt's neck responded, "*Chhoto*Ma isn't going to eat. You go away."

Rebuking him, Annapurna shouted, "Shut up, you! This little boy is at the root of all the trouble. What a spoiled brat you are making him with your over indulgence, *chhotobou*! You'll realize it later and then you'll tearfully regret and say that didi had warned you long ago!"

Bindu whispered something into Amulya's ears and he repeated it aloud, "Why don't you leave, didi? *Chhoto*Ma is telling me fairy tales."

Scolding again Annapurna affirmed, "You'd better get up, *chhotobou*, if you know what is good for you! Otherwise, if I don't send you both away you might as well call me by any other name but Annapurna." Saying which, she went out with the same heavy footsteps as she had come in earlier.

Madhab asked, "What happened between the two of you today?"

Bindu answered, "The same thing that happens when *didi* gets angry and nothing more. The only offensive thing I told her today was that, since there is a child in the house, things like nutcrackers and all should be kept with care. That is what is causing all this uproar."

Madhab advised, "Don't make anymore fuss, please go."

The way *bouthan* was thumping her feet *dada* would get up any minute.

Bindu, taking Amulya in her arms, smilingly went to the kitchen.

## *Three*

These two mothers spent six more years depending on the only child in the same way two sons grow up, depending on their common mother. Amulya was now a grown up boy, studying in the second grade of the high school. There was a tutor in the house engaged to coach him. After he had finished studying with him in the morning Amulya went out to play. It was a Sunday and there was no school.

Entering the room Annapurna asked, "*Chhotobou,* tell me what shall I do?"

Bindu, taking out all of Amulya's garments from the wardrobe and piling them on the floor, was selecting one set of clothes for him to wear. He was to go with his uncle to a rich client's home for some kind of event. Without lifting her face up, Bindu asked, "About what, *didi*?"

Bindu was not in a good mood. Annapurna was astonished to see the extent and variety of Amulya's garments and so she did not notice the expression on Bindu's face. Keeping silent for a few moments she asked, "Are all these Amulya's clothes?"

Bindu answered, "Yes."

Annapurna responded, "How much money can you waste! The cost of any one of them could pay for the clothes of the son of a poor man for one whole year."

Bindu was annoyed but she responded in a normal tone, "It may be so. But there will always be some difference between the rich and the poor. There is no point in feeling sorry for it, *didi*."

Annapurna commented, "You may be rich but you go overboard in everything."

Lifting her face up Bindu asked, "I don't have much time on my hand, didi. Tell me what is on your mind."

"When did you ever have time to spare, *chhotobou*?" Saying which, she left in a huff.

Bhairab went to find Amulya and bring him home. After searching for about an hour he found him.

Bindu asked, "Where were you for so long?" Amulya remained silent.

Bhairab responded, "He was playing tip-cat with the peasant boys from the other neighborhood."

Bindu was fearful of this game and she had forbidden him to play it. So she said, "Didn't I forbid you to play tip-cat?"

Amulya turning blue in fear responded, "I was just standing there. They forced —."

"Did they force you? Well, you are going out now. I'll deal with it later." Saying which, she began to dress him up.

Amulya had his *sacred thread* ceremony about two months earlier. He violently objected to wear the gold-thread-embroidered cap on his hairless head. But Bindu was not the kind of a person to let it go. She forced it on his head. Amulya, wearing the gold-thread-embroidered cap on his bald head, began to sob.

As Madhab was entering the room he asked, "How much longer will he take to get ready?"

Then, as he noticed Amulya, he exclaimed with laughter, "Well, well, he looks like King Krishna Chandra of Mathura!"

In utter embarrassment Amulya threw away the cap and fell on the bed, face down.

Piqued, Bindu responded, "As it is the child was crying and you—"

Becoming somber Madhab commented, "Don't cry Amulya, get up. If anyone is labeled as *gone out of his mind* it will be I. Now, you come with me."

The same comment had been made on an earlier occasion and Bindu was outraged by it. Repetition of the same comment made her being on fire. "I do everything like a crazed person, is that right?" So saying she dragged Amulya out of the bed and gave him a few blows with the handle of the hand-fan and then began to peel off the expensive velvet robe from Amulya.

Fretful Madhab went out to inform Annapurna, "*Bouthan,* she has gone out of her rocker, please go."

Entering the room Annapurna found that Bindu had already taken out all the expensive garments and was putting on some very simple clothing. Amulya was standing there, utterly wan faced out of fear.

Annapurna said, "He was looking great. Why did you take them off, *chhotobou?*"

Bindu, letting Amulya go and suddenly wrapping the edge of her sari round her neck, said with folded palms, "I beseech you *baroginni,* please go away from here. All of your interventions will beat the living daylights out of the poor boy."

Annapurna stood there speechless.

Bindu, pulling Amulya by one ear and making him stand in a corner of the room asserted, "Your punishment must fit your crime. You will remain locked up in this room all daylong. *Didi,* come out. I am locking up this room." So saying, she came out and pulled the chain up.

Around one o'clock, Annapurna could not keep quiet any longer. She said, "*Chhotobou,* really won't you let Amulya eat anything today? Will all the people in the house go on fasting because of him?"

Bindu answered, "That depends on the people in the house!"

Annapurna told, "What kind of a talk is this, *chhotobou?* He is the only child in the house. If he goes without food how can even the maids and servants eat, let alone, You or I!"

Stubbornly Bindu responded, "I know nothing about that."

Annapurna realized that any amount of arguing would not cut it. So she pleaded, "I am asking you to listen to your elder sister. Forgive him for this time. Besides, if he becomes sick it is you who is going to suffer."

Thinking of how far the day had advanced Bindu herself was getting soft. She called Kadam and told, "Go and fetch him here. But I am also telling you all, didi, the consequence of going over my head will not be good."

The turmoil ended there for the day.

As his younger brother became well established in his law practice, Jadab retired from his work and looked after the family's assets. The ten thousand rupees that the *chhotobou* brought into the family had almost doubled with earned interest. Taking a portion of that money and depending on his brother's income he had been building a large house a quarter of mile away for the past year. It was about ten days the house was completed. It was agreed that after the Durga Puja[1] was over all of them would move into the new house on some auspicious day. So one day while Jadab was eating his meal he addressing *chhotobou* said, "The construction of your house is complete, Ma. One of these days you must go and see if anything has been overlooked."

Bindu had one habit. In the midst of a thousand chores she always stood behind the door while her elder brother-in-law ate his meals. She respected her brother-in-law like a god — as everyone else did. Bindu stated, "Nothing has been overlooked."

Laughing, Jadab responded, "You gave the verdict even without seeing it Ma! Very well indeed! But there is one more thing on my mind. It is my desire that we bring all our relatives here. Then we all move over there on an auspicious day and worship the family deity all together. What do you say, Ma?"

Bindu said softly, "Let me consult with *didi*. Everything will be done following her opinion."

Jadab responded, "You may do that. But you are the Lakshmi, the goddess of bounty, in my family, Ma. All work will be done according to your will."

Annapurna was seated nearby. Laughing she commented, "If only your Ma Lakshmi was a little calm in her disposition."

Jadab added, "What do you mean by *calm in her disposition*, *barobou*? My Ma is like the Divine Mother Jagadhatri! She bestows boons and if needed she uses her weapons too. I want her just like that. Since she came into our family we never had the slightest want and suffering."

---

[1] Worship of the Supreme Mother Goddess, mostly by the Bengalis, in the autumn.

Annapurna affirmed, "You have said the truth. I still feel fearful to think of the days before her coming into the family. "

Feeling abashed Bindu, putting a lid on that sort of talk, said, "Please bring all the relatives. That house of ours is big enough for everyone. No one will have the slightest discomfort. They can stay for two or even six months if they so wish."

Jadab affirmed, "That will be done, Ma. I'll make all the arrangements tomorrow."

## *Four*

Their cousin, Elokeshi, (a sister from father's side), was not in good financial condition. Jadab often used to send her financial assistance. For a while she had been writing about her desire to keep her son, Naren, here for his education. On this occasion she appeared with her son from Uttarpara. No one could say for sure what her husband, Priyanath, did there. He, too, came within a day or two. Naren was sixteen or seventeen years old. He used to wear wide-bordered-*dhotis*[1] with a circuitous fold and comb his hair at least eight to ten times a day. The parting of his hair was really something to behold. Today all of them were sitting on the verandah of the kitchen and Elokeshi was describing her son's uncommon beauty and qualities.

Bindu asked, "Which grade you are in now?"

Naren answered, "In the fourth grade — Royal Reader, Grammar, Geography, Arithmetic, and much more like decimals and such other stuffs which you will not understand, *mami*[2]."

Taking one look at her son's face with pride Elokeshi told Bindu, "It is not a matter of one or two books, *chhotobou*— it is a veritable mountain! Why don't you, my darling, take the books out of the box tomorrow and show them to your *mami*?"

Nodding his head Naren replied, "Very well, I'll show."

Bindu commented, "He has a long way to go yet for his graduation."

Elokeshi explained, "There should not have been any delay at all, *chhotobou*. By this time he would have graduated not once or twice

---

[1] The loin-cloth worn by all respectable Hindus of North-India. It is rapped round the body, waist down, the end being then passed between the legs and tucked in at the waist, so that a festoon of calico hangs down to either knees.

[2] The wife of a maternal uncle, an aunt.

but at least four times. But it hasn't happened entirely due the mean-minded teacher. May utter misfortune strike him. Only he knows why he sees my gem of a son with such an evil eye. Does he allow him to progress to a higher level? No, never! Out of sheer spite he is keeping my son in the same class, year after year."

Astonished Bindu said, "I never heard of such a thing happening."

Elokeshi responded, "Doesn't happen? It happens all the time! All the teachers are in it together. They want bribes! I am a poor person. You tell me from where can I find the money to bribe them?"

Bindu remained silent. Feeling sincerely sorry Annapurna commented, "Isn't it terrible to harass people in this manner? Is it good conduct? But we don't have these things here. Our Amulya brings home good books as prize every year. We don't have to bribe anyone."

Just at that moment Amulya came from somewhere and sat down on his *chhoto* Ma's lap. Twining his arms around her neck he whispered to her ear, "*Chhoto* Ma, tomorrow is Sunday, Please ask Master Mashay to go away today."

Laughing, Bindu said, "This boy you see, *thakurjhi*[1], can't be taken away from where stories are being told. Kadam, go and tell Master Mashay that Amulya won't study today."

Astonished, Naren opined, "What is this, Amulya? You are a grown up boy now and still you sit on the lap of a woman!"

Laughing, Bindu responded, "That is not all he does! Still at night—"

Embarrassed Amulya, covering her mouth with his hand, begged, "Don't tell, *chhoto* Ma, don't tell!"

Bindu didn't divulge but Annapurna did. "He still sleeps with *chhoto* Ma at night," she told.

Bindu said, "It is not only that he sleeps, didi, but also hangs on like a bat."

Embarrassed Amulya buried his face in his *chhoto* Ma's bosom.

---

[1] A sister of one's husband, a sister-in-law.

Naren exclaimed, "Shame! Shame! What are you! Do you study English?"

Annapurna answered, "Certainly he does. He studies only English in the school."

Naren commented, "I don't believe he studies English! Let me see. Can he spell *Injin*? He can never do that."

Elokeshi added, "That is a very hard word. How can a little boy spell that?"

Annapurna cajoled, "Why don't you do it, Amulya?"

Amulya could not be made to lift his face.

Pressing his head upon her bosom Bindu said, "How can he spell if all of you embarrass him?"

Looking at Elokeshi she continued, "He will have his first graduation next year! Our Master Mashay has assured us that he would get a scholarship of twenty rupees. And with that money he will buy a pair of horses like his uncle has."

Though the statement was true yet everybody took it as a joke and laughed.

Addressing Bindu, Elokeshi added, "My Narendranath is not only good in his studies but also he is so good in theatre that people can't hold back their tears. Why don't you show your *mamis*, dear, the way you said it all when you were dressed as Sita?"

At once Naren fell on his knees and started to say in a nasal tone, "Lord of my heart! In what an inauspicious moment this slave of yours—"

Fretful Bindu implored, "Stop! Stop it! And keep quiet. *Batthakur* is there upstairs." Startled Naren stopped.

Annapurna was charmed by these few words. She commented, "Let him do the speech about gods and goddesses! It is very good indeed, *chhotobou*."

Annoyed, Bindu asserted, "Then you can listen about gods and goddesses. We are leaving."

Naren added, "Then let me do the part of Savitri."

Bindu was emphatic, "No!"

Hearing Bindu's tone Annapurna came to her senses. She could understand that the matter has gone too far and it is not going to end here. Elokeshi was a newcomer. She did not understand what was behind all this. So she said, "You stop here for now. You can do it some day in the noon hour when the men will be away. His ability in vocal and instrumental music is no less. Sometime you can do that weeping song of Damayanti. Once your *mamis* hear it they would never let go of you."

Naren added, "Shall I do it right now."

Bindu was seething with anger. She said nothing.

Annapurna was quick to say, "No! No! There is no need for singing now."

Naren responded, "Very well then. I'll teach the song to Amulya. I can play on the drum too. *Mami* it is very difficult to play *tere kete taak* rhythm cycle. If you will pass me that brass jar I can show you."

Signaling Amulya to get up Bindu said, "Amulya, go to your room and study."

Amulya was spellbound to hear all this. He didn't want to get up. He said in a hushed voice, "Why don't you stay a little longer, *chhoto* Ma."

Without saying a word Bindu made Amulya get up and she went to her room taking him with her. Annapurna understood why she suddenly left like that. She became concerned that Bindu was not likely to agree to the idea of Naren staying here for his studies, lest Naren become a very negative influence on Amulya. She said, "Naren, dear, don't do your acting and such things in your *chhoto* mami's presence. She gets irritated easily and she is not fond of these things."

Surprised, Elokeshi said, "*Chhotobou* doesn't like these things! That's why she left like that."

Annapurna responded, "It may be so. There is something else you should keep in mind, dear. You are here for your room and board and study. You should do things that would lighten the burden of your mother's hardship. You shouldn't be too close to Amulya, dear. He is a little boy, much younger than you."

Elokeshi did not like the advice. She said, "That is right. My son comes from a poor household and he should behave like an impoverished boy. But since you raised the issue let me say something, *barobou.* Is Amulya a green little child and is my Naren a ripe old man? The difference of a year or less does not make one young and the other old. And do you think that he has never seen a wealthy man's son in his life? There are many sons of the likes of kings in his theatre party!"

Embarrassed, Annapurna asserted, "No *thakurjhi*, I didn't mean that. I wanted to say —"

"What else did you want to say, *barobou.* We may not be smart but we are not so stupid that we don't understand it! But dada let us to believe that Naren would stay here to study. That's why we came here. Otherwise weren't we surviving there?"

Annapurna, shrinking into herself in embarrassment, responded, "God only knows *thakurjhi*, I didn't say that at all. I only talked about lightening the burden of mother's hardship and —"

Elokeshi replied, "Very well, let it go at that. Go Naren and you can sit outside the house. Don't you come close to a wealthy person's son." Saying which, she pushed her son out and she went away at the same time.

Storming into Bindu's room and almost sobbing Annapurna said, "Because of you do we have to cut off all ties with relatives? Tell me why did you leave the place?"

Bindu calmly said, "*Didi*, there is no need to cut off ties. You live happily with all the relatives and let me flee from this place with my son. That is it!"

"Where are you going to flee?"

Bindu answered, "Don't worry. I'll leave you the address on the day of my departure."

Annapurna quipped, "I know that. You won't stop until you have done something that would make it impossible for us show our faces in public. All my life I have suffered untold misery with this *bou.*" So saying she was about to leave when finding Madhab entering the room she was in flames again, "*Thakurpo*[1], either you live in some other place or you send this *bou* somewhere for good. I'm telling you clearly that I won't be able to keep her here any longer." Saying which, she left.

Dumbfounded Madhab asked, "What's the matter?"

Bindu answered, "I don't know. But since *baroginni* has decreed you can now banish us."

Madhab did not say anything. He picked up the newspaper from the table and left the room.

[1] A younger brother of one's husband, a brother-in-law.

## *Five*

Though *thakurjhi* appeared foolish in her demeanor yet it would a mistake to underestimate her. As soon as she found out that the childless Bindu was loaded with money she at once was on her side and she began to upbraid her husband every night saying, "It is for you that I lost everything. Instead of uselessly staying with you if I would have stayed here I would have been the mother of a king today. Instead of my golden moon-like son that ghost-like dark son — *chhotobou* never would have — ." Saying which, she would release a long and dispirited sigh, as if to end the life span of the black-ghost. Then she would conclude by saying, "The poor have God on their side," and turning to one side she would sleep. Priyanath, too, would repent for his stupidity and fall asleep. The couple spent their days in this way and *thakurjhi's* love and affection for *chhotobou* were swelling up like floodwater.

At midday today, she was saying, "I have never seen you braiding your hair, which is like the dark monsoon clouds. The ladies from the *zaminder's* home are coming for a visit. Come and let me braid your hair into a bun."

Bindu responded, "No, *thakurjhi,* I can't keep my sari on my head all the time. My son is grown up now and he will notice it."

Astonished, *thakurjhi,* claimed, "What kind of a talk is that, *chhotobou*? Just because a son has grown up a married woman would not braid her hair? My Narendranath, (and may woe come to his enemy), may be older than he by six months or a year. And should I stop making buns on my head for that reason?"

Bindu responded, "Why should you stop *thakurjhi?* Naren has seen it all his life. He is different. But Amulya will gawk at my head to find, all of a sudden, a braided bun on my head. He might even scream or do something else. Shame on me. That would be highly embarrassing!"

Suddenly Annapurna was passing by. Looking at Bindu she stopped in her tracks and said, "Why are your eyes glistening, *chhotobou*? Come to me and let me feel your body temperature."

Bindu, feeling very much abashed in Elokeshi's presence, responded, "Why should you feel my body-temperature everyday? Am I a little girl that I won't know it myself if I am sick?"

Annapurna retorted, "No, you are very old. Come to me. This is *Bhadra/Ashwin*[1] season and it is a very bad time."

Bindu insisted, "I'll never come. I am telling you that nothing is wrong and still you are asking me to come to you!"

Annapurna responded, "Don't you mislead me!" she left, looking at her with suspicious eye.

Elokeshi commented, "It seems *barobou* suffers from some phobia."

Bindu remained still for a moment and then added, "*Thakurjhi*, may all have a little bit of that kind of phobia!"

Elokeshi remained silent.

Annapurna, with something in her hand, was returning the same way. Calling after her Bindu asked, "*Didi*, listen to me! Will you braid your hair into a bun on your head?"

Turning around Annapurna stood there. Gazing in silence for a moment or two and comprehending the whole matter she told Elokeshi, "*Thakurjhi*, it is futile to talk to her about it. She has so much hair but she won't tie it in a bun, she has so much clothes and jewelry but she won't wear them and she has so much beauty but won't even take care of it. Her mentality is bizarre. And the son is also taking after her. Do you know, *chhotobou*, what Amulya told me the other day? He said what was the use of wearing so many garments? *Chhoto*Ma has so many clothes but does she wear them?"

Lifting her face up and laughing with pride Bindu affirmed, "Now, don't you see, *didi*, that a mother has to have this type of bizarre mentality to make her son a cut above the rest! Should you live that long didi, you'll see people, pointing at you, declaring —

---

[1] The sixth month of the Bengali calendar and the second month of the two months of post-rainy season, from mid- August to mid-September.

there goes Amulya's mother." As she was saying her eyes became filled with tears.

Noticing that Annapurna affectionately said, "And for that reason we say nothing about your son. May God fulfill your heart's desire! But we don't hold such high hope that your son will become a very important person, one special one among the many!'

Wiping her eyes with the edge of her sari Bindu responded, "But didi, I am living only with that hope. My God!" All of a sudden it made her hair stand on end. Embarrassed, Bindu continued with folded palms, "No, didi! I'll go mad if anything would stand in the way of my hope."

Annapurna became speechless. It was not that she was unaware of what was in the heart of her younger sister-in-law. But she never realized so vividly such high hopes and aspirations within her own self before. Today she became conscious why Bindu was ever vigilant like the demigods, guarding heaven's treasures and ever cautious like a specter! Looking at the face of all embracing well-wisher of her son, her motherly heart became filled with an in explicable respect and tenderness. She turned her face the other way to hide the tears about to overflow her eyes.

*Thakurjhi* said, "It may be so, *chhotobou*, today your —"

Interrupting her, Bindu quickly said, "Yes, *thakurjhi*, make a braided bun on *didi's* head today. I've never seen it since the day I came into this house." Saying which, she left with a teasing smile on her face.

One morning, five or six days later, the long standing barber of the household, after shaving Jadab, was coming down the stairs. Amulya, blocking his way, asked, "Kailash da, can you give hair cuts like that of Naren da?

The amazed barber answered, "How is that my little master!"

Amulya, pointing to different parts of his head told, "Look, it is this way — twelve annas here, six annas there, two annas over there and very short on the back of my head. Could you cut it like that?"

Laughing, the barber responded, "No, my little brother. Not even my father could do it."

Amulya did not give up. Encouraging him he showed again, "It is not difficult at all Kailash da, twelve annas here, six annas there, —"

The barber, thinking of a way out, suggested, "But what day is it today? Unless your *chhoto* Ma commands me I can't do it."

Amulya replied, "Very well! Please stay here. Let me find it out." But just after taking one step and coming back he said, "Give me your umbrella, otherwise you might flee." So saying and snatching the umbrella he ran away. After storming into the room he asked, "*Chhoto* Ma, would you come quick for a minute?"

*Chhoto* Ma had just finished taking her bath and she was about to sit down to say her prayers to God. Being concerned she retorted, "Don't touch me, don't touch me! I am saying my prayers."

"You can say your prayers later *chhoto* Ma; please come out and give him the order otherwise he won't cut my hair. He is waiting!"

Bindu was a little surprised. It had always been a hassle to give him haircut. She couldn't figure it out why he was so eager to cut his hair today. But as soon as he came out the barber said, "He has given me a challenging order, Ma. I have to cut his hair like Naren Babu[1] — twelve annas, six annas, four annas, two annas and so on — would I be able to do that?"

Amulya said, "You'll be able to do that quite easily. Wait a minute, let me get Naren da here," and he ran out. Searching for him for a while and coming back, he said, "He is nowhere. Let that be. *Chhoto* Ma, stay here and show him. Look at me carefully — twelve annas here, six annas there, two annas over here and very short over there. "

Observing his enthusiasm Bindu said laughing, "I am to say my prayers now!"

"You can say your prayers later, otherwise I will touch you."

Finding no other way Bindu had to wait there.

---

[1] A term of respect attached to a name, like Master or Mr. Instead of addressing a Bengali gentleman as Mr. X (the surname) it is a common practice to address as X-babu (where x is the first name). In the days of the East India Company the clerks in offices were called Babu by the British and even today a supervisory clerk is called Baro-babu. Baro meaning the big(boss).

The barber began to cut his hair. Bindu winked her eyes. He cut all the hair to the same length. Amulya felt his hair with his hand and being delighted, "This feels all right." Then he happily galloped away.

Taking his umbrella under his arm the barber remarked, "Ma, it will be hard to enter this house tomorrow."

*Bamunthakrun*, after getting his food ready, was calling out for him. Bindu, sitting in a corner of the kitchen and getting the milk ready could hear that Amulya was looking for his uncle's brush all over the house. Coming back after a while and leaning on Bindu's back he said, "He has done nothing right, *chhoto* Ma. He has ruined everything. I'll kill him tomorrow."

Bindu couldn't control her laughter. Moving away from her back he said, "Are you blind? Can't you see anything?"

Hearing him cry and coming into the room Annapurna heard the whole story and said, "That is nothing serious! Tomorrow I'll ask him to cut it the way you want."

Getting even angrier Amulya replied, "How it can be twelve annas here? Where is the hair for it?"

To console him Annapurna added, "It may not be quite twelve annas but it might be eight or ten."

"Absolutely nothing will come off it. Is eight or ten annas any fashion? Go and ask Naren da — it has to be twelve annas!"

That day Amulya did not eat his meal adequately. Scattering his food all around he went away.

Annapurna asked, "Since when did your son get the idea of a fancy hair cut?"

Bindu laughed. But, becoming somber in the next moment and releasing a disparaging sigh she said, "I laughed because it is a trifling matter. But I am becoming scared to death because everything begins in this manner."

Annapurna couldn't say anything more.

Durga Puja was at hand. Entertainment galore was arranged in the zamindar's house in the other neighborhood. Naren was totally absorbed in it for the past two days. On the *Saptami*[1] night Amulya entreated, "*Chhoto* Ma, a country-opera is going on. Shall I go to see it?"

*Chhoto* Ma answered, "Is it going on now or will start later?"

Amulya responded, "Naren da said that it would begin at three o'clock."

"You will stay all night in the dew? That can't be. You can go with your uncle tomorrow morning. You will have a good seat for viewing."

Almost on the verge of crying Amulya pleaded, "No, send me now. Uncle might not go and even if he goes it might be quite late."

"If it starts at three or four o'clock I'll send you with a servant. Now sleep for a while."

Piqued, Amulya moved to a corner of the bed and lay down, facing the wall.

As Bindu tried to draw him close he moved her hand away and lay down there, stiffening himself. Perhaps all of them fell asleep then for a while. At the sound of the clock outside restless Amulya got up from his sleep. Paying keen attention he began to count — one – two – three – four – getting up in a hurry and shaking Bindu with all his might he said, "Up, up, *Chhoto* Ma. It has already struck three or four!" The clock outside continued to strike – five – six – seven – eight – sobbing, Amulya added, "it has struck seven or eight. When shall I go?" The clock outside still continued to strike –nine – ten – eleven –twelve – and then it stopped. Recognizing his own mistake embarrassed Amulya lay down silently. Madhab used to sleep on a bed on the other side of the room. He was also awakened by the noise.

Laughing aloud, he asked, "Amulya, what happened?"

Embarrassed, Amulya did not respond. Laughing, Bindu commented, "The way he woke me up people wouldn't do so even if the house were on fire." Noticing Amulya silent her heart melted. She said, "Well you can go now. But don't get into a fight with anyone."

---

[1] The seventh day of a lunar fortnight.

Then after sending for Bhairab she sent Amulya with a light. At about ten o'clock in the morning, after happily returning home and seeing his uncle he at once said, "Didn't you go?"

Bindu inquired, "How was it?"

"The country-opera was splendid, *chhoto* Ma. Uncle, there will be *khemta*[1] dance in the evening. Two professional dancers have come from Kolkata. Naren da has seen them — they are very beautiful, just like *chhoto* Ma. They will dance. I have told baba[2] too."

"Well done!" Saying which, Madhab burst out laughing.

Bindu's face was flushed in fury. "Listen to the comment of your nephew, the bag of all qualities!"

Then she bawled at Amulya, "You'll not go there again, even for once, you wicked scoundrel! Who said they look like me, Naren?"

With a trembling heart Amulya responded, "Yes, because he has seen them."

"Where is Naren? Let him come!"

Controlling his laughter Madhab said, "Are you out of your mind! *Dada* has heard it too. Don't make any more fuss about it." So, swallowing the insult Bindu began to boil within.

Just before the evening Amulya came to Annapurna and implored, "*Didi*, I want to go to see dance in the Puja-place. I'll just see the dance and come back immediately."

Annapurna, busy with her work, responded, "Go and ask your mother."

Amulya began to insist, "No, didi, I'll be back right away. Please say that I can go."

Annapurna reaffirmed, "No, that can't be. She has bad-temper. You tell her and then go."

Amulya began to sob and pull her sari, "Please don't tell *chhoto* Ma. I am going with Naren da and I'll be back shortly."

Annapurna told, "If you are going with Naren —"

---

[1] A kind of dance with a specific rhythmic measure.

[2] Another word for father like papa, daddy for English speaking people.

Amulya didn't let her complete the sentence when he ran out very fast.

An hour or so later the word came to Annapurna that Bindu was looking for him. She remained silent. The search for Amulya intensified. Then coming out she said, "Some dancing or something is going on. He has gone with Naren to watch that. He'll be back soon. You have nothing to fear."

Coming close Bindu asked, "Who permitted him to go, you?"

Annapurna could not disclose this, out of fear that he had gone without consent. So she said, "He'll be back soon."

Bindu left with a gloomy face. After a while, as soon as Amulya entered the house, he heard that *chhoto* Ma was looking for him. At once he went to his father and lay down in a corner of his bed.

· With his reading glasses tied to his eyes Jadab was reading the Bhagabad under an oil lamp. Lifting up his face he asked, "Who is it, Amulya?"

Amulya did not respond.

Coming there Kadam announced, "*Chhoto* Ma is calling you, come."

Coming close to his father he pleaded, "Baba, why don't you come along?"

Perplexed, Jadab asked, "I have to come along! What is the matter Kadam?"

Kadam explained it all.

Jadab understood that some altercation was inevitable. One person has forbidden and the other has permitted. So he came along with Amulya and calling after *chhotobou,* from outside her room he spoke, "Forgive him for this one time, Ma. He is promising not to do it again."

That night when the two sisters-in-law sat down for dinner Bindu said, "I am not upset with you didi, but I don't think that I can stay here with Amulya any longer. Amulya will soon be totally out of control. It would be a different matter if I hadn't forbidden him. Since that time I have been pondering where did he find the courage to do it in spite of my specifically forbidding him. Then think of his contemptible scheme! He didn't come to me. Instead he went to you. When he came and heard that I was looking for him he brought *batthakur* with him. No didi, until now he never behaved in this manner. I would rather live with him in a rented place in Kolkata. That would be much better than seeing my only son amounting to nothing and I shedding tears all my life."

Feeling distressed, Annapurna responded, "Tell me, should you go away how would I live all alone?"

Remaining silent for a moment or two Bindu answered, "You should know that. I just told you what I would do. That Naren is a very bad one."

"Why, what did Naren do? Suppose, they were brothers. What would you have done in that case?"

Bindu answered, "Then I would have a servant tie his hands and feet and rub nettles drenched with water all over his body and throw him out of the house. Besides, there is no use in talking hypothetically. You would do better to get rid of them."

Annapurna felt irritated. "Whether they should be abandoned or not is not within my control. You ought to tell him who got them here in the first place. It is useless to reproach me."

"How could I tell *batthakur* all these things?"

"The same way you talk about other things."

Pushing away the platter of food Bindu responded, "Don't take me for a simpleton, didi. I am also going to be twenty-seven or twenty-eight. This is not about maids or servants in the house. It is about relative. Wouldn't *batthakur* take umbrage of my talking about it as long as you are alive?"

Annapurna retorted, "Certainly he will. But if I should tell he would never see my face again. After all we are outsiders and they are brother and sister. Shouldn't you think of that? Besides, I am an old hag and if I would make a fuss about such a trivial matter wouldn't people call me crazy?"

Pushing away the platter of food even further away Bindu sat there with a gloomy face.

Annapurna reasoned to herself that Bindu was keeping quiet out of fear of her elder brother-in-law. She said, "What offence did the food platter commit that you are not eating."

Suddenly Bindu let out a deep sigh and said, "I have finished eating."

Observing her mood Annapurna didn't dare to insist anymore.

Going to her bed to sleep and not finding Amulya there Bindu came back to ask, "Where did he go?"

Annapurna answered, "I saw him sleeping in my bed. Let me go and wake him up."

"No, no! Let him be there." So saying, Bindu went away with a wan face.

Around midnight Bindu woke up from her light sleep when Annapurna called after her from outside the door.

"What's the matter didi?"

Annapurna responded from outside, "Open the door and take your son. Even my father wouldn't be able to tolerate his naughtiness!"

As Bindu opened the door, Annapurna, along with Amulya, came in and she continued, "I've seen many scoundrel boys but never one like him, *chhotobou.* It is now about two o'clock and he never even let me have a wink of sleep! First he is hungry, then mosquitoes are biting him, then he must have a drink of water and then I have to fan him —no *chhotobou,* I work all day long and I can't survive if I can't sleep at night."

As soon as Bindu smilingly opened her arms Amulya slipped into her lap and burying his face in her bosom fell asleep in a moment.

Madhab, jokingly quipped from his bed on the other side, "*Bouthan,* has your fancy been satisfied?"

Annapurna retorted, "It was not my fancy. He himself went there out of fear of his mother. And I have learnt the lesson of my life. And what a disgusting thing he said, *thakurpo,* that he is ashamed to sleep with me."

The three of them laughed. Annapurna said, "No more, let me have a little sleep." Saying which, she left.

About ten days later Bindu's parents, intending to go on a pilgrimage and wishing to see their daughter before their departure, sent a palanquin to bring Bindu. Taking consent of her elder sister-in-law, Bindu, keeping it a secret from Amulya, was preparing to visit her parents for two or three days. Just at that time, carrying his schoolbooks under his arms and before leaving for school, Amulya appeared. A little while earlier he had seen a palanquin by the roadside. All of a sudden, taking one look at her feet, he froze and asked, "Why you have applied *alta*[1] on your feet, *chhoto* Ma?"

Annapurna was present. She could not help but laugh.

Bindu responded, "It has to be worn today."

Amulya, repeatedly scrutinizing her from head to foot asked, "Why have you put on so much jewelry?"

Annapurna, covering her moth with the edge of her sari, left the place.

Bindu, controlling her chuckle, answered, "Can no one wear jewelry? Must I leave it for your wife to wear them someday? Now go to your school."

Amulya, paying no heed to it, questioned, "Why is *didi* laughing so much? I am not going to school but where are you going?"

Bindu answered, "Even if I were to go somewhere do I have to get your permission?"

"I, too, will go." Saying which, he went out with his books.

Entering the room Annapurna commented, "I never thought that he would go to school so easily. Did you notice how sharp he is? So many questions —why you have applied *alta,* why you are wearing jewelry? I still ask you to take him along. Otherwise, after returning from school and not finding you home, he'll create a riot."

Bindu responded, "*Didi*, do you think he has gone to school? Not on your life! He must be hiding somewhere and he'll appear at the right time.

---

[1] A deep red paint used by Indian women to decorate the borders of their feet.

Precisely that is what happened. He was in hiding. After taking the dust from Annapurna's feet the moment Bindu was about to get into the palanquin Amulya, appearing from somewhere and holding the edge of her sari, stood there. The two sisters-in-law burst into laughter.

Annapurna said, "Don't lash out at him at the time of your departure. Take him with you."

Bindu responded, "I can take him this time, *didi.* I can't take one step without him. This is becoming a serious matter."

Annapurna added, "He has become exactly what you have shaped him into. Amulya, why don't you stay with me for a couple of days."

Shaking his head Amulya retorted, "No! No! I won't stay with you." Saying which, he got into the palanquin first.

## *Six*

One midday, about ten days after Bindu had returned from her parents' home, as Annapurna was entering her room she called after her, "*Chhotobou?*"

*Chhotobou* was sitting motionless with a pile of soiled clothes in front of her.

Annapurna asked, "Has the washerman come?"

*Chhotobou* did not utter a word. Observing the mood reflected in her visage Annapurna got really scared. Being worried, she asked, "What is the matter?"

Pointing with her finger at two pieces of burnt cigarettes Bindu said, "They came from Amulya's shirt pockets."

Annapurna stood there speechless.

All of a sudden bursting into sobs, Bindu pleaded, "I beseech you, *didi*, either you send them away or send us somewhere."

Annapurna could find no answer. She stood there in silence for a while and then went away.

In the afternoon, after returning from school and eating his snacks Amulya went out to play. Bindu did not say a word. The servant, Bhairab, came to complain. Though he did nothing wrong Naren Babu slapped him."

Irritated Bindu said, "Go and tell it to *didi*."

Returning from the court, Madhab, as he was getting out of his office clothes made a small joke. He was at once silenced by a sound rebuff. Only Annapurna could feel the severity of the storm, unbeknown to others, that was gathering in the house. Spending all evening in anxious restlessness and finding Bindu alone she clasped the palms of *chhotobou* with her hands and entreated her, "When all are said and done he is your son after all! Forgive him this time. Better yet, take him aside and chastise him severely."

Bindu responded, "He is not my son. I know it and you know it too. What's the use of such futile talk, *didi*?"

Annapurna answered, "It is not I. You are his mother. I gave him to you."

"When he was a little boy I fed him and looked after him. Now he has grown up. You take your son and relieve me of the burden." Saying which, Bindu went away.

In the night Amulya, with a long face, came to Annapurna to sleep.

Understanding his motive and getting annoyed she rebuked, "Why have you come here? Go away from here. Go!"

Turning around he found his father asleep. He went away slowly without uttering a word.

Next morning, when Kadam came into the kitchen to pick up the dirty dishes and utensils from the previous night, she found Amulya sleeping on a pile of firewood and dung-cakes. She ran and got Bindu. Annapurna was also just awakened from her sleep. Coming close she stood there.

In a very sharp tone Bindu said, "Probably *baroginni* threw him out last night. Her sleep gets disturbed if he is there. Isn't that so?"

Seeing the condition of her son Annapurna felt remorseful and aggrieved. Her eyes were brimming over with tears. Unable to stomach Bindu's cruel rebuke she flared up, "You find relief in piling your faults on someone else's shoulder."

As she was picking up her son Bindu felt that his body was hot — he had fever. She said, "It is inevitable that he would have fever lying like this in the cold in the month of *Kartik*. I only hope that he recovers."

Anxious Annapurna, bending low, commented, "Let me see if he has fever!"

Bindu, pushing her hand away rather forcefully, affirmed, "Leave him alone. There is no need for you to examine him." Picking up her sleeping son with ease and casting one venomous look at Annapurna she went into her room.

Though Amulya recovered within five or six days Bindu could not forgive her elder sister-in-law's offense. From that day she could not even talk to her in a civil manner.

Annapurna, in her mind, understood everything. Yet she also remained silent. She could not forget that Bindu had publicly put the blame on her alone. One day, during her conversation with Elokeshi on some other matter she had stated, "His fever is entirely due to *chhotobou's* fault. It is his good fortune that he did not die."

Elokeshi lost no time to tell Bindu the same. Bindu listened to it attentively but made no comment. No one but Elokeshi knew that Bindu was aware of Annapurna's remark. Bindu stopped talking to her elder sister-in-law altogether.

Household effects had been moved into the new house for the past few days. Next morning was the time for the final move. Jadab, along with all the male members, were in the new house. Madhab was away in connection with some court case. Meanwhile a very serious incident happened in the old house.

The tutor had come in the evening to teach. "From tomorrow you'll teach him in the new house," she said.

The tutor said, "As you wish." As he was leaving Bindu asked, "How is your student studying these days?"

The tutor replied, "He has always been good in his studies. He stands first every year."

Bindu responded, "That he does all right. But he has learnt to smoke cigars now!"

Perplexed, the tutor retorted, "Has he learnt to smoke cigars?"

Then he added, "It is not surprising. Boys learn everything from others."

"Learnt from whom?"

The tutor remained silent. Bindu added, "Please make his father aware of it."

Shaking his head the tutor said, "Consider this: It happened about five or seven days back. While going to school they invaded the orchard of a man from Orissa. They stole his out-of-season mangoes, broke tree branches and even beat the poor man — all in all it was a veritable mess."

Holding her breath Bindu asked, "And then?"

The man from Orissa complained to the Headmaster. He mollified the man by imposing a fine of ten rupees on the boys.

Bindu found it difficult to believe. She asked, "Was my Amulya involved in it? Where would he get any money?"

The tutor responded, "I don't know that. But he was in it. Naren Babu of this household was also involved along with three or four notorious boys from the school. I have heard this from the Headmaster Mashay."

Bindu asked, "Has the money for the fine been already paid?"

"Yes, Madam! I have heard that too."

"Well, you can go now." So saying Bindu sat down right there. These words barely came out from her lips, "Giving him money without my knowledge! Who can have so much courage in this house?" As it is she was in a depressing mood, she was not in talking terms with her didi and above all this incident made her to lose all sense of right or wrong conduct.

Getting up she went into the kitchen. Annapurna was cutting vegetables for the nighttime meal. Lifting her face she looked at the dark-cloud-covered-face of *chhotobou.*

Bindu asked, "Didi, did you give any money to Amulya recently?"

Annapurna was dreading this very thing. Her throat became bone dry with fear. Softly, she asked, "Who said that?"

Bindu responded, "That is not important. What is important is this: what reason did he give you and how did you justify giving it?"

Annapurna remained silent.

Bindu continued, "You don't want me to discipline him. That's the reason for you concealing it from me. Whatever Amulya might do he would never lie to his respected elders. You gave him the money with full knowledge of the reason. Isn't it true?"

Annapurna responded softly, "True, please forgive him for this time, dear, I am begging your pardon."

Bindu's heart was on fire. She retorted, "This time! From today I forgive him forever. I'll say no more. I'll never butt in. I won't be able to tolerate that he will, little by little, go to the dogs right before my eyes. It is better that I let go of him at once. But think of your audacity!"

The last word hurt Annapurna deeply. Yet she sat there silently. But the more Bindu rambled on the more her fury increased. She again thundered, "Every time feigning ignorance you say — forgive him this time. But his guilt is not as much as yours. I'll never forgive you."

The maids and the servants in the house were listening to all of it, staying out of sight.

Annapurna could not tolerate it any more. She retorted, "What will you do? Hang me from the gallows?"

Oil was poured into fire. Bindu exploded like spark in gunpowder, "That would be the appropriate punishment for you."

"I gave two rupees to my own son. Isn't that my crime?"

One thing led to another. Forgetting about the right issue these words spilled out of Bindu's mouth, "Why should you even do that? Where does the money to waste come from?"

Annapurna shot back, "Don't you waste money?"

"I waste my money. Tell me, whose money do you waste?"

This outraged Annapurna very much. She came from a poor household and she thought to herself that Bindu was hinting at that. Standing up she answered, "You may come from a very wealthy family but you should not have the vanity to think that no one else can even spare two rupees!"

Bindu responded, "I don't have that vanity. But you should think when you spend even one penny whose money you spend."

Annapurna thundered, "Whose money do I spend? Do you say whatever comes to your mind? Go away from my sight."

Bindu responded, "Go away! I'll do that as soon as the night will end. But can't you see whose money you spend? Don't you know whose income pays for your living expenses?"

Having said these words abruptly Bindu stopped and became silent.

There was not a trace of blood on Annapurna's face. Staring unblinkingly for a moment or two at the face of *chhotobou* she responded, "We are living on your husband's income. I am your maid and a slave. He is your servant! Is that what you mean to say? Why didn't you say this for so long?"

Her lips quivered again and again. Biting on her lips and remaining motionless for a moment she asserted, "Where were you, *chhotobou*, when my husband could not afford to have two pieces of cloth at one time because of paying the expenses of educating his younger brother? Where were you when after the old house burned to ashes, he stayed under a tree and ate one meal a day, cooked by himself? That is how he rebuilt this ancestral homestead."

As she was speaking tears were raining from her eyes. Wiping her eyes with the edge of her sari she continued, "If he ever knew what was in your hearts he would never have spent his days in comfort, closing his eyes, intoxicated with opium and smoking the hookah pipe. He is not that kind of a person. Your husband knows him and the gods in heaven know him too. You insulted him, using me as the pretext!"

Annapurna's chest began to heave with pride in her husband. She added, "It is a good thing that you expressed it clearly. Sati committed suicide to hear her husband's humiliation. I, too, am taking a vow: I would rather support myself by working as a cook somewhere but I would never take a grain of your food. What have you done today? You have humiliated him!"

Just at that moment Jadab, entering the courtyard called out, "*Barobou*!"

At the sound of her husband's voice her feeling of hurt, shame and embarrassment became uncontrollable like a stormy ocean. Coming out running she told, "Shame! Shame on you! Why can't a man who can not feed his wife and son, can't even find a rope to hang himself?"

Perplexed, Jadab answered, "What happened now?"

"What happened? Nothing at all! *Chhotobou* spelled it out today: I am her maid and you are her servant."

Inside her room Bindu bit on her tongue and plugged her ears with her fingers.

Sobbing, Annapurna continued, "I have no right to give even a paise to anyone. I had to swallow this insult while you are alive. I am taking this vow today in your presence that I shall eat their food over my son's dead body."

These words entered Bindu's plugged ears indistinctly. Somehow muttering, "What did you do, didi!" she sank into herself. Bindu suddenly fainted and fell on the floor after twelve long years.

## *Seven*

Every one, except Jadab, Annapurna and Amulya, came to the new house. From far away Bindu's *pishi*[1], her daughter, grand children, and from her parent's home her parents, maidservants and maids-in-waiting — all had filled the home. Bindu was absentminded the day she came to the new home. But she got over it the next day. Bindu didn't have the slightest doubt that Annapurna would come after her anger subsided. There will have to be the worship of the deity of the house and a feast for all. Bindu got busy in making arrangements for all these events.

Bindu's father asked, "Ma, why haven't I seen your son?"

She briefly responded, "He is in the other house."

Her mother asked, "Is it that your sister-in-law could not come?"

Bindu answered, "No!"

Her mother added, "If everybody would come here who would be left there? You can't just abandon the ancestral homestead."

Bindu went to do her work.

Every evening Jadab used to come to check everything, and get all information. He would sit outside but never ventured in. The night before the worship of the house-deity, going inside, he sent for Elokeshi and he was inquiring about everything. Getting wind of it Bindu began to listen to everything, remaining unseen by them. From early on until just the other day she received so much affection from this elder brother-in-law, who was more than a father to her. How affectionately he called her; always "Ma" and never even *bou* Ma. How many times, after a tiff with her sister-in-law she had complained about her and she was never ignored. Today her limitless

---

[1] A sister or a cousin sister of one's father, an aunt.

shame choked her voice in his presence. Jadab went away. Inside the room, all alone, stuffing her mouth with her sari, lest the people in the house could hear her, she began to cry her eyes out.

Next morning, sending for her husband she said, "The day is wearing on and the priest has been waiting but *batthakur* has not yet come." Puzzled, Madhab replied, "Why has he to come?"

Even more puzzled, Bindu retorted, "Why he has to come? Who else is going to do all these?"

Madhab answered, "Either I or Priya Babu, the brother-in-law. *Dada* won't be able to come."

Piqued Bindu responded, "How can you say that he won't be able to come? As long as he is alive no one else has the right to do it. No! No! That won't do. I won't let anyone but him do anything."

Madhab added, "Then let us stop everything. He is not home, for he has gone to work."

"This is *baroginni's* doing. Then she won't come too, I presume." Saying which, she left with a face about to break into tears. To her all the arrangements, festivities, worship, grand feast — all became hollow in a moment. For the past three days she had been thinking every moment that today *batthakur* would come, didi would come and Amulya would come. No one but she knew how much hope was riding on today's daylong festivities and how much she thought to herself of being relieved by depending on them for everything. As soon as that one comment from her husband made everything vanish like a mirage the whole futile workload of festivities seemed to descend on her chest like a heavy stone.

Coming in Elokeshi said, "*Chhotobou,* give me the key to the storeroom. The confectioners are here with the *sandesh*[1]."

Exhausted, Bindu said, "Keep it somewhere for now, *thakurjhi,* I'll take care of it later."

"Where shall I keep them *bou,* the crows would get at them."

"Then throw them out." So saying she left for another place.

*Pishima*[1] came in to ask, "Can you show for once how much wheat flour is to be used for making dough now."

---

[1] A kind of sweetmeat made of posset.

Bindu responded with a glum face, "How should I know how much wheat flour will be needed? You are experienced homemakers. Don't you know how much?"

Surprised, *pishima* answered, "Pay attention to what you are saying. How should I know how many people you are expecting for this meal?"

Enraged, Bindu said, "Then go and ask my husband. *Didi* was somebody! At the time of Amulya's *sacred thread* ceremony people of this town had their meals for three consecutive days. Did she ever ask, '*chhoto bou,* do this, look after that!' All the people of this house can't even match one bone of her body to get things done." So saying she left for another room.

Coming in Kadam asked, "*Jamai* Babu was inquiring about the clothes for the *puja* —"

Before she could finish talking Bindu screamed at her, "Why don't you all eat me up! Be off with you from my sight."

Kadam fled in a hurry.

A little later Madhab, coming in and calling after her several times said, "Do you hear me, dear?"

Coming close Bindu thundered, "I don't hear, I can't hear and I'll not hear. Does that satisfy you?"

Puzzled, Madhab, kept on staring at her.

Bindu continued, "What will you do? Hang me by the neck? That would be better!" Saying which she hurriedly left, weeping.

The day wore on even longer.

Restless Bindu was going from one room to another without any specific purpose and finding fault with people. Someone in a hurry had left some utensils on a walkway. Jerking and scattering them all over the courtyard Bindu taught them the right way to work. Someone had left some wet clothing to dry. As one garment touched her body she taught them how clothes should be dried by shredding the offending piece. Whoever happened to be on her path stood aside out of fear.

---

[1] A sister or a cousin sister of one's father, an aunt.

The hapless priest himself coming inside commented, "The day is well advanced but I see no arrangement —"

Bindu, remaining unseen said rudely, "Some delay is inevitable when so many things are going on." Saying which, she kicked an utensil out of her way and going into another room sat there exhausted. About ten minutes later on hearing a very familiar voice she hurriedly stood up. Looking out through the door she saw Annapurna coming into the courtyard and standing there.

Bindu broke into sobbing from hurt, shame and embarrassment. Wiping her tears, coming close and facing her she wrapped the edge of her sari round her neck and with folded palms she said, "Now it must be ten or eleven o'clock. How much more enmity will you do with me, *didi*. If my drinking of poison will fulfill your desire then you can go home and send me a bowl-full of it." So saying she threw the bunch of keys noisily at her feet and locked herself in her room. Lying down on the floor she began to cry.

Annapurna silently picked up the keys and entered the store room.

In the afternoon the visiting and feasting was on the wane; still Bindu was listlessly going from one room to another with something on her mind.

Bhairab came and informed, "Amulya Babu is not in the school."

Bindu looked at him with flaming eyes and roared, "You wretched fellow! Do the boys stay in school until nighttime? Are you a newcomer here? Couldn't you go to the other house and take a look there?"

Bhairab added, "He is not in that house too."

Bindu shouted, "God knows where he is, playing tip-cat with some lowly boys. He is no more afraid of anyone. *Baroginni's* heart's desire will be fulfilled if he would be blind in one eye! Then she would happily eat with ten hands. — Go and find him wherever he may be!"

Annapurna, sitting in front of the storeroom was talking to a few elderly ladies. She heard *chhotobou's* shrill voice.

About an hour later Bhairab came back and told, "Amulya Babu is in the house but he did not come." Bindu could not believe him.

"What do you mean — he did not come! Did you tell him that I sent for him?"

Bhairab, shaking his head said, "Yes! Still he did not come."

Bindu, keeping quiet for a moment, added, "It is not his fault. Like mother like son! I am also taking a vow: I won't see the faces of such a mother and her son."

When the night was far advanced and Annapurna was getting ready to leave, Madhab, himself, came to escort her.

Bindu hurriedly approaching them boomed, "You are going to escort her. But are you aware that she didn't even take a sip of water?"

Madhab answered, "You are supposed to know that. It is not my job. Noticing that everything was going to waste I brought her over myself and now I am taking her back myself too."

Bindu responded, "Very well indeed! I see that you are also on that side."

Madhab, without answering, said, "Let's go, *bouthan*, don't wait any longer."

"Let's go *thakurpo*." Saying this, as Annapurna took one step forward, when Bindu thundered, "It is for nothing that people say blood-feud! You told a pack of lies in whatever way you felt like, then you took a series of harsh vows, for four days and four nights you did not let me see my son — God will be your judge."

Saying which she stopped her cries by pushing the edge of her sari into her mouth. Coming onto the verandah of the kitchen she fell on her face and fainted. A clamor ensued. Both Annapurna and Madhab heard it. Annapurna, turning around said, "Let me see what happened."

Madhab responded, "There is no need to see. Let us go."

For a long time the feud was under cover but now it didn't stay that way. The next day when all the women were sitting together Elokeshi spoke out, "The two sisters-in-law quarreled but what happened to the son? Couldn't he come at least once? *Chhotobou* didn't say any untruth — like mother like son! I have seen many boys but never an ungrateful one like him."

Bindu, giving her a tired look, lowered her head in shame and disgust.

Elokeshi continued, "You love boys, *chhotobou.* Take my Narendranath. I am giving him to you. You can beat him up, even cut him too — but he will never talk back. We don't bear that kind of a son."

Bindu sat there silently. The response came from her mother. She was well advanced in her age. She was the daughter of a zamindar and the wife of one too and she was one with experience. She said with a smile, "What kind of a talk is that. Amulya is part and parcel of her being. Don't make her bewildered like that. Bindu, your tiff will last only a few days, dear and can that sever the bond between you and your son?"

With her eyes brimming over with tears, and looking at her mother's face, Bindu sat there in silence. In the evening sending for Kadam she asked, "Well Kadam, you were present on that day. What a big offence did I commit that she had to take such a serious vow?"

Kadam could not easily believe that Bindu had sent for her to discuss this matter with her. Cringing into herself she sat there in silence.

Yet Bindu continued, "No! No! After all you are older than I and I have to listen what you say. Tell me what a big offence did I commit?"

Shaking her head Kadam answered, "No, *didi*, it was not such offence!"

"Then why don't you go to their home now and tell them off as they deserve. You have nothing to fear."

Gathering some courage Kadam answered, "I am not afraid, didi. But what is the use of getting into a new altercation. Whatever had to happen has happened."

Bindu responded, "No! No, Kadam! You don't understand that it is better to tell the truth. Otherwise, she'll think it is all my fault and that she did nothing. Didn't she say that she would throw me out, she would send me away? Did I ever get upset at these? Why did she give him money behind my back? Why didn't she tell me just once?"

Kadam suggested, "Very well, I'll go tomorrow. It is now already evening."

Displeased, Bindu asserted, "Do you think that it is evening? You argue too much! It looks dark because it is late in the winter afternoon. You take someone with you. Oh, Bhairab, do you hear me? Send for Hebo and let him go with Kadam."

Bhairab replied, "Babu is getting the lamps cleaned by Hebo."

Raising her eyebrows Bindu rebuked, "Again you are talking back to me!"

Bhairab moved away very fast from that look. After sending Kadam away and going into this and that room a few times Bindu entered the kitchen. The Bamunthakrun was cooking there, all alone. Sitting down beside her Bindu said, "Very well, you good woman, you are my witness! Tell me the truth — who is more guilty?"

Failing to understand the question the cook asked, "About what, Ma?"

Bindu answered, "About the happenings of the other day! What did I say? I merely inquired, '*Didi*, have you given Amulya any money recently?' Everyone knows you don't just hand out money to children whenever they ask. She could have said, 'Amulya was badgering me and so I gave him.' That would have been the end of it. Isn't so much talk and taking vows totally uncalled for? When a bunch of utensils are kept together they sometimes bang on one another, and in this case we are talking about human beings! Does that call for such a serious vows? That too about the only scion of the lineage! I am telling you, good woman, I'll never see her face as long as I live. I'll look at my enemies but never at her."

The *bamunthakrun* was by nature a woman of few words. She kept quiet.

Bindu's eyes were filled with tears. Wiping her tears quickly she continued in a wistful tone, "She didn't even take a sip of water! Didn't even let the son come! Is this the right conduct for an elder person? After all I am young and have less experience. Suppose I was her daughter, then what she would have done? You watch me, I'll never utter her name even."

The *bamunthakrun* still kept quiet.

Bindu continued, "She is not the only one who can take a vow? Can't I do the same? If I go to her home tomorrow and tell her that if she wouldn't send me a cup of poison the same vow will apply to her — then what would she do? I am keeping quiet for the past two days. Now I'll go there and take the same vow, or better yet I will take a cup of poison myself and tell everyone that *didi* sent it. Wouldn't people speak ill of her and wouldn't that be some tit for tat!"

Getting scared *bamunthakrun* said softly, "No, Ma! Don't even think of such ideas. Altercations, feuds don't last forever. She won't be able to live without you and your Amulyadhan also won't be able to live without you. We have been wondering how he is surviving the past few days!"

Distressed Bindu responded, "You said it right, good woman! I am sure he has been beaten and made to stay there under duress! The one who can't sleep even one night without me has by now spent five days and four nights without me! Can one cast even one glance at such a woman! I said it already that I would rather look at my enemy but never at her as long as I live!"

Showing a black mark on her wrist *bamunthakrun* added, "Look here, Ma. The black mark is still there. When you fainted that night Amulyadhan, coming from somewhere and falling on your bosom, how hard did he cry! He had never seen you like that before. So he thought that his *chhoto* Ma had died! He wouldn't let any one sprinkle water on your face or fan you. When I tried to pull him away he bit me. When *baro* Ma tried to pull him away he scratched and bit her and made a mess of her sari by tearing it. At last it took four or five people to drag him away."

Bindu, stared at her face with unblinking eyes as if she was gulping every word. Then releasing a long dispirited sigh and getting up slowly she went into her room, shut the door and slept.

About four days later, and the day before Bindu's father, mother, *pishi* and other people were to leave, Bindu, regaining consciousness after another fainting spell, was lying quietly in her bed. Kadam was fanning her and there was no one else there. Bindu, signaling her to come even closer, asked softly, "Kadam, has *didi* come?"

Kadam answered, "No, *didi*. So many of us are here and why give her trouble?"

Keeping still for a moment or two Bindu responded, "This is what is wrong with you people, Kadam. On the day of the Puja a house-full of people were there. But could you do anything until that little person stepped in? All of you on one side and she alone — there is no comparison. A house-full of you people can't even match her little finger in skill!"

Entering the room, Bindu's mother said, "My son-in-law has given his consent for your coming with us for a few days of change of air."

Staring at her mother Bindu responded, "Does my going or not depend on his consent, Ma, that I can go because he has said so? How can I go without the permission of my sworn enemy?"

Understanding whom she meant her mother opined, "When you have separated from them his permission is good enough."

Shaking her head Bindu added, "No, Mother, that can't be. As long as she is alive she is supreme. Whatever I can do, Ma, I can't leave this house without her permission. *Batthakur* will be upset."

Elokeshi had just come there and heard it. "Well, I am telling you. You can go."

Bindu didn't even respond to her.

Her mother suggested, "Very well then. Why don't you send someone to ask her permission."

Puzzled, Bindu responded, "Send someone? That would be even worse, Ma. She would say, 'Let her go.' But in her heart she would remain angry. Perhaps she would fabricate stories to tell *batthakur*. No, Ma. You all can go. I can't go anywhere."

Her mother did not insist anymore. Now the empty house seemed to be ready to swallow her at every moment. Elokeshis lived in one room on the ground floor. Only one room on the second floor was for her use and the rest of the house was stark empty. Roaming through the house with a vacant mind she came into a room on the third floor. She had intended this room as the living quarters of her son and daughter-in-law in some distant future. On entering this room she could not hold back her tears. While coming down the stairs as she met her husband she cried out, "Then how would it be possible, dear?"

Failing to understand what she meant Madhab asked, "What?"

Bindu could not respond. Suddenly, letting out a deep sigh she said, "No, no! You can go. It is nothing."

Next morning Madhab was busy with his work in the outer room. Suddenly entering the room and holding back her tears she asked, "Is it true that he is working?"

Without looking up he replied, "Yes."

"How can you say, yes! Is it right for him to work at his age?"

Keeping his eyes on his work Madhab answered, "People do not work because the age is right. They work to meet their needs."

"Why should he need to work? We are outsiders and we have quarreled. But aren't you his brother?"

Madhab retorted, "Only a step brother — a mere relative."

Astounded, Bindu said slowly, "As long as you are alive will you let him work?"

Now looking up at his wife Madhab said in a calm and collected manner, "Why wouldn't I let him work? I am a living example of the saying that everyone comes into this world with predetermined destiny. I don't even know when my father died. I used to hear from *bouthan* that we were very poor but I never experienced even a wisp of pain and suffering that goes with poverty. Even to this day I can't figure out from where I always got clean and crisp clothes, the fees for school and college education, the books, and my living expenses for staying away from home. I haven't have a shabby income since I became a lawyer. Meanwhile you came from somewhere with a pile of money and now we have this palatial home. At the same time take a look at dada. All his life he has always silently worked his fingers to the bone, had worn stitched and tattered clothes and had only one meal a day so that we would have a good life. I can't remember it all and don't see the need to remember it either. He had enjoyed a little comfort for a while and God is making him to pay for it through his nose." Saying which he turned around and began to search for an important piece of paper.

Bindu was speechless and motionless. Every drop of blood in her body could feel the severe reprimand by her husband that was hidden behind the simple story of bygone days. Bending her head low she stood there.

While searching for the paper, Madhab, as if talking to himself, added, "It is no easy job! It is in the office of the zaminder of Radhapur, a walking distance of over ten miles in coming and going. He leaves at four o'clock in the morning and stays without any food all day long and eats only one meal at night — and his salary is only twelve rupees a month."

A shiver ran through Bindu's entire body. "Without any food for the whole day! Only twelve rupees!"

"Yes, only twelve rupees. He is quite advanced in his age. Besides, as an opium addict he doesn't even get a little milk that he needs. It seems to me that God has, after so long, mercifully given him a way to end his worldly suffering.

Tears began to rain from Bindu's eyes and she did something that she had never done before. Bending her head down and clasping her husband's two feet she begged, as she wept, "I beseech you and beg you. Please find a way. He is a person in ill-health and he won't survive such hardship more than a few days."

Wiping his own tears strenuously Madhab responded, "How can I find a way? *Bouthan* would not accept even one grain of food from us and how can they survive without some kind of help?"

Bindu entreated in a chocked voice, "I know nothing about that. My dear, you are my god and his place is higher than that of yours. How can I utter something that I am ashamed even to think—" Bindu could not say anymore.

Madhab advised, "Very well, then, at least go to *bouthan.* Do something that would pacify her anger and please her. Otherwise there will be no solution even if you sat here all day, clasping my feet."

Bindu at once letting go of his feet and sitting up said, "It is not in my habit to clasp anybody's feet. It is now clear to me why she didn't take even one sip of water on that night and knowing it all you kept silent as if you were my enemy. The load of my offence increased and you said nothing!"

Madhab put his mind to his papers and added, "No! I have learnt it from dada. God willing, I hope to leave this world someday without expressing my feelings."

Bindu said nothing more. Going to her room she locked herself there.

Madhab was about to get up when Bindu again came into the room. Her two eyes were blood-red. Feeling compassionate Madhab urged, "Go to her, just for once. You know her well. Just stand before her and all will be resolved."

Bindu begged in a pitiful tone, "Please, you go! I beseech you in the name of my son—"

Reading her mind Madhab, becoming a little displeased, responded, "Even if you beseeched me a thousand times I can't approach dada. Unless he asks me himself I can't talk to him about it. I won't dare to do it even at the cost of my life."

Still Bindu did not move.

Madhab pleaded, "Couldn't you go?"

Bindu did not answer. Lowering her head she slowly walked away.

## *Eight*

The road to the school ran in front of the house. The first few days Amulya, hiding his head with his umbrella, went to the school along this road. For the past two days the umbrella, sailing on this road, was not visible. Tears rolled down her cheeks as Bindu watched and watched the road for a long time. Yet, sitting on the roof top, she kept a steady vigil. From nine to ten in the morning many boys went along the road with their many colored umbrellas. The same boys returned along the same road after the school break. But Bindu did not see that familiar way of walking or that familiar umbrella. Wiping her eyes dry and coming down in the evening she called Naren aside and asked, "Naren, this is the shortest way to the school. Then why doesn't he go to the school along this road?"

Naren remained silent.

Bindu added, "Isn't it nice that the two of you, brothers, will go to school and come back together, taking about so many things!"

Naren had loved Amulya in his own way. He whispered, "*Mami*, he doesn't go along this road out of shame. He takes the round about road away over there."

Bindu responded with a strenuous smile, "Why should he be ashamed? No. no! You tell him to go this way."

Shaking his head Naren asserted, "He'll never go this way, *mami*. Do you know why he won't go?"

Anxious, Bindu asked, "Why?"

Naren said, "Promise you won't be angry?"

"No!'

"You won't send anyone to their house to tell it?"

"No!"

"You won't tell even my mother?"

Impatient Bindu responded, "No, I won't! You can tell me and I won't tell any one."

Naren whispered, "The third Master severely boxed Amulya's ears!"

Bindu flaring up for a moment like fire said, "Why did he do that? Didn't I forbid them to touch his person in any manner?"

Waving his hand he replied, "He is not to be blamed, he is new to the school. Our servant, that bastard Hebo is the devious one. He told my mother. My mother is no less devious either. She asked him to tell the Master. And the third Master at once boxed his ears. Do you know, *mami*, how hard did he box his ears? In this way, grabbing his—"

Stopping him in a hurry Bindu asked, "What did Hebo say?"

Naren answered, "You know it *mami* that Hebo takes my lunch everyday. He came running and asked, "What kind of food Naren da?" On hearing this, Ma said that Amulya had cast his evil eye on my food."

"Doesn't anyone take lunch for Amulya?"

Naren, touching his forehead with his hand in desperation answered, "Where would they get it *mami?* They are too poor! He takes a few roasted chick peas in his pocket. During lunch time he eats those, hiding under a tree on the other side."

The house and everything else began to wave before Bindu's eyes. Sitting down on the floor she said, "Naren you can go now."

That night, after much cajoling and sitting down to eat Bindu could not bring her hand to her mouth. In the end she got up on the pretext that she was not feeling well. The next day also she ate almost nothing and she could not tell anything to anyone. Neither had she found any solution. She was constantly afraid that if any one knew of it her offence would increase even more. By force of habit she sat near her husband during his afternoon meal but she turned her face away from the food. Since the day before she could not bear to look at any kind of food.

The lamp was burning in the room. Madhab, with his eyes closed, was stretched out on the bed. Coming in Bindu sat near his feet. Looking at her Madhab asked, "What is it?"

Lowering her head down Bindu was scratching one of her husband's nails.

Presuming what was on his wife's mind Madhab's heart softened, "I understand it all, Bindu. It is futile to cry before me. You go to her."

Bindu was indeed crying. She begged, "Please, you go."

"I will go to plead for you. Won't dada hear about it?"

Without answering directly she added, "I am telling you that I am the guilty one. I am begging their pardon. Please, you tell it to them."

Saying, "I can't do it," Madhab turned away to sleep.

Hoping against hope Bindu sat there for a long time. But when Madhab didn't say a word she slowly left. Her husband's conduct, in a moment, spread from one end of her heart to the other end like a vast rock-solid rebuke. That day she realized it without any doubt that everybody had abandoned her.

The next morning Jadab sent a letter, giving her permission to go to her parents' home. Bindu's father was ill and she must go without any delay. With her eyes brimming over with tears Bindu got into the carriage.

The *bamunthakrun*, coming close to the carriage said, "After your father's recovery, please come back as soon as you can, Ma."

Getting down from the carriage, as Bindu was about to take the dust of her feet the *bamunthakrun* moved away and shrank into herself.

No one had ever seen Bindu so polite and humble. Taking the dust of her feet Bindu said, "No! Good woman, after all you are a Brahmin's daughter and also older than I. Bless me that I don't have to come back and let this be my last journey."

The lady cook could not say anything in response — Looking at Bindu's wan and washed out face she began to sob.

Elokeshi was present there. She admonished in a shrill voice, "What kind of a talk is that, *chhotobou*. Don't other people's parents become ill?"

Bindu didn't answer. Turning her face away she wiped her tears. After a few moments she said, "I bow to you too, *thakurjhi*. I am now on my way."

*Thakurjhi* responded, "Go *didi*, go. I am staying here to look after everything."

Bindu did not say anything anymore. The coachman started the carriage.

Hearing all these events from *bamunthakrun* Annapurna remained silent.

Bindu had never before gone to her parents' home without Amulya. It was now more than a month that she hadn't had a glance of him. Annapurna could fathom the depth of her sorrow.

Lying near his father Amulya was talking softly.

Sitting on the floor and under the light of a lamp Annapurna was sewing a patchwork cotton-quilt. Suddenly releasing a dispirited long sigh she commented, "Bless her soul! At the time of her departure she had wished this to be her last journey. By the grace of Mother Durga may my dear one come back in good health."

Hearing it and sitting up Jadab responded, "*Barobou,* you haven't done the right thing from the very beginning. None of you really appreciated my Ma!"

Annapurna affirmed, "She too didn't come to her *didi* even for once! She could have insisted to take her son. But she didn't even do that! After working hard all day long when I was returning home that night, on the contrary, she made so many harsh comments!"

Jadab added, "Only I understand the meaning of what my Ma says! But, *barobou,* what's the use of your being the elder one if you can't forgive this much? You and Madhu are of the same kind. I am afraid that, in the end, the two of you would kill my Ma!"

Tears began to pour from Annapurna's eyes.

Amulya asked, "*Baba*, why did *chhoto* Ma say that she won't come back?"

Wiping her tears Annapurna asked, "Would you like to go to your *chhoto* Ma?"

Shaking his head Amulya answered, "No."

"Why won't you go? Your *chhoto* Ma has gone to your grandparent's home. Why don't you go there tomorrow?"

Amulya kept quiet. Jadab asked, "Would you go Amulya?"

Burying his head in the pillow and shaking his head like before he answered, "No!"

Jadab used to get ready for work while there was a little night left yet. At such a time, five or six days later, after getting ready for work he was smoking the hookah absentmindedly.

Annapurna commented, "It is getting late for you."

Leaving the hookah aside and standing up restlessly Jadab commented, "Today my mind is restless, *barobou.* Last night my Ma came and she was waiting behind that door." Uttering, "Durga! Durga!' he left for work.

In the morning, tired Annapurna was working in the kitchen. The servant from the other house gave the news, "Babu left for Pharashdanga last night. Ma is seriously ill." Remembering her husband's parting words Annapurna's heart cried out. "What sort of illness?" she asked.

The servant answered, "I don't know that for sure. But I heard that after a few fainting spells it has taken a serious turn."

Returning home after the evening and listening to the news Jadab, bursting into tears, said, "With high hopes I got a golden goddess for the home and you immersed her in water, *barobou.* I'll go right now."

Annapurna's heart was almost shattered in grief and remorse. She, perhaps, loved *chhotobou* more than even Amulya. Wiping her own tears and washing her husband's feet she almost forced him to sit for saying his prayers to God. Then she sat in the verandah in the dark. A little later Madhab's voice was heard. Making her heart as strong as possible and plugging her ears with her fingers she sat there like a rock.

Finding the kitchen dark and coming back to the main house he saw Annapurna sitting there in the dark. "Perhaps you have heard *bouthan*," he said dryly.

Annapurna could not lift her face.

Madhab continued, "For once, Amulya should go. It appears the end of her journey is near."

Falling on the ground Annapurna broke down completely. Distressed Jadab came running from the other room. "This can not be happening Madhu!" he asserted, "I am telling you it can never happen! Consciously or unconsciously I have never caused any heartache to anyone. God can not inflict such punishment on me at my age."

Madhab remained silent.

Jadab said, "Tell me everything in detail. I'll bring back my Ma. Don't you be overwhelmed with grief, Madhu. Do you have a carriage with you?"

Madhab responded, "I am not overwhelmed, dada. But what are you doing?"

"I have done nothing. Get up *barobou*, come along Amulya —"

Interrupting him Madhab suggested, "Let the night pass dada."

"No, no! That will not do. Don't be overwhelmed, Madhu. Call a carriage now or I am walking."

Without saying anything else when Madhab got a carriage the four of them got into it. Jadab asked, "What happened?"

Madhab answered, "I wasn't there and so I don't know for sure. I was told that after high fever about four days back she had repeated fainting spells. Since then no one has been able to feed her a drop of milk, let alone any medicine. I can't say for sure what has happened but there is no hope."

Jadab emphatically affirmed, "There is plenty of hope. Hundred times! My Ma is alive. Madhu, God will not make me tell lies at this fag end of my life. So far I have never told a lie."

Madhab, at once taking some dust from his elder brother's feet on his head, remained seated in silence.

***Nine***

No one knew for how long Bindu was causing the deterioration of her health by starvation. She had fever after she had come to her parent's home. On the second day she fainted two or three times. She was not regaining consciousness after her latest fainting spell. After much effort when her consciousness returned her pulse could hardly be felt. Madhab arrived after getting the news. She took the dust of her husband's feet but kept her teeth clenched together. Even after endless entreaties she did not even take a drop of milk.

Disappointed, Madhab asked, "Why are you committing suicide?"

Tears began to stream along the corner of her eyes. After a little while she said softly, "Amulya gets everything that I have. Give only two thousand rupees to Naren and see that he gets education. He loves my Amulya."

Biting his lips Madhab controlled his tears.

Bindu, signaling him to come even closer, whispered, "See that no one else but him does my last rites."

Controlling even that shock Madhab whispered to her ears, "Do you wish to see anyone?"

Shaking her head Bindu responded, "No, let it go."

Bindu's mother tried to give her medicine once more. But she kept her teeth firmly clenched.

Standing up, Madhab asserted, "I won't let that happen, Bindu. You didn't listen to any of our entreaties but I am going to get the one whose command you can not ignore. Keep only this plea of mine: I want to see you alive when I return." So saying Madhab came out and wiped his tears. That night Bindu slept peacefully.

The sun was just rising. Madhab entered the room and put out the lamp. As soon as he opened the window Bindu opened her eyes.

Looking at her husband in the morning's gentle light she asked with a gentle smile, "When did you come?"

"Just now! *Dada* is weeping like a man out of control."

Bindu said gently, "I can very well imagine. Did you bring a little dust of his feet?"

Madhab responded, "He is sitting outside and smoking hookah, *bouthan* is freshening up and Amulya fell asleep in the carriage. He is sleeping upstairs. Shall I wake him up?"

Remaining still for a moment or two she said, "No, let him sleep." Saying which, she turned to her side and lay down, facing the other way.

Annapurna entered the room and sat near her head. She touched her. Bindu was startled. In a minute or so Annapurna regained control over herself and said, "Why didn't you take any medicine, *chhoto*? Do you intend to die?"

Bindu didn't answer. With her lips to Bindu's ear Annapurna whispered, "Do you realize that my heart is shattering into pieces?"

Bindu whispered back, "I do, *didi*."

"Then turn your face this way. Your *batthakur* has come himself to take you home. Your son has fallen asleep crying. Listen to me, turn your face."

Still Bindu didn't turn her face. Shaking her head she said, "No *didi*, first you say —"

Annapurna responded, "I am telling you just that, *chhoto*. Only you do come back home, just once."

Just at that moment as Jadab stood in the doorway Annapurna pulled the bed sheet over her head. For a moment Jadab looked at his dear *chhotobou*, covered from head to foot and on whom he doted immensely. Controlling his tears he said, "Let us go home, Ma. I have come to take you there."

Looking at his wan and washed out face tears came to the eyes of everyone present. Keeping silent for another moment Jadab continued, "On another occasion when you were a mere girl I came to take the goddess of bounty of my home. I never thought that I would have to come again. When I have come, Ma, then you listen to my words: either I am going to take you with me or else I would never go back that way. You know it, Ma, that I do not lie!"

Madhab went out.

Bindu, turning her face around said, "*Didi*, give me whatever you want to feed me. And then bring Amulya to lie down beside me and you all can go out of this room and take some rest. You don't have to be afraid anymore — I'll not die."